The Abingdon Preaching Annual 2021

The Abingdon
Preaching
Annual

2021

**Planning Sermons and Services
for Fifty-Two Sundays**

Tanya Linn Bennett, General Editor

Nashville

THE ABINGDON PREACHING ANNUAL 2021:
PLANNING SERMONS AND SERVICES FOR FIFTY-TWO SUNDAYS

Copyright © 2020 by Abingdon Press

ISBN 978-1-5018-9663-7

20 21 22 23 24 25 26 27 28 29—10 9 8 7 6 5 4 3 2 1
MANUFACTURED IN THE UNITED STATES OF AMERICA

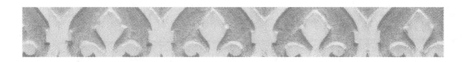

Contents

LECTIONARY SERMON AND WORSHIP HELPS

Contents

🌿 = Sunday in Lent   ✪ = Sunday of Advent

ESSAYS FOR SKILL-BUILDING

Lectionary Sermon and Worship Helps

January 3, 2021–Second Sunday after Christmas Day

Jeremiah 31:7-14 or Sirach 24:1-12; Psalm 147:12-20 or Wisdom of Solomon 10:15-21; Ephesians 1:3-14; John 1:(1-9) 10-18

Jennifer Quigley

Preaching Theme

Because of the timing of Christmas this year, there is space in the lectionary for a Second Sunday after Christmas on January 3 before the Epiphany on January 6. Even if your church does celebrate Epiphany a bit early on this Sunday, keeping these lectionary readings, with their focus on wisdom, will enrich your church's Epiphany celebrations.

This Sunday includes some unusual texts that rarely appear in the lectionary. We find two texts from the Apocrypha: **Sirach** and the **Wisdom of Solomon**. While Protestant Christians have had a variety of perspectives on how to think about the Apocrypha, Christians throughout history have found meaning and wisdom in these books. I like the way that the Greek Orthodox Church refers to these texts; rather than quibble over their precise theological importance, they simply call them *anagignoskomena*, or "worth reading." These texts *are* worth reading, especially because they help us to consider a theme we do not notice in **John 1**, a text which is so familiar to us: the theme of wisdom. At a time when so much human knowledge is a quick internet search away, what does it mean to think about wisdom?

Sirach is a Jewish book, written in Hebrew and translated into Greek about two hundred years before the life of Jesus. Sirach is a collection of instructions and proverbs, but in this passage, we hear Wisdom speaking amid God's people. This text likely reminds us of **Proverbs 8**, where Wisdom is described as present alongside God at the beginning, participating in all of creation. Sirach, too, envisions Wisdom as taking root in a particular way among God's people.

The Wisdom of Solomon is a Jewish text written in Greek about one hundred years before Jesus. The Wisdom of Solomon is addressed to the rulers of the earth, exhorting them to rule with justice and equity. The "She" of this text is also Wisdom, and again we are reminded of Proverbs 8. Here, Wisdom is described as the abiding presence of God among God's people, as the cloud and pillar of fire guiding the Israelites in the wilderness, as the compass steering them through the Red Sea.

Reading these two texts helps us notice the ways in which the Gospel of John's author also seems to have Proverbs 8 in mind. The prologue of John's Gospel describes *Logos*, often translated as *Word*, which is in the beginning with God and *is* God. *Logos* has a wide range of meanings, though, and can encompass written words, speech, thought, reason, and even wisdom. God, in **Genesis 1**, after all, creates through speech. John 1 then, for all its emphasis on Jesus as the Word that is made flesh, is also trying to tell us something about Jesus as Divine Wisdom.

It might seem disjointed to jump from reading about Jesus as a helpless infant lying in a manger to reflecting about wisdom. These readings remind us that Divine Wisdom, the Word, is present with God at the beginning of everything and is beyond our possible understanding. At the same time, that Divine Wisdom dwells in a special way among God's people by taking on our humanity in the person of Jesus. It is precisely in that tension that the mystery of the incarnation lies.

This is a tension that Hildegard of Bingen, a Benedictine abbess, musician, and writer, captures in her hauntingly beautiful chant about wisdom: "O virtus Sapientiae." Wisdom, she writes, has three wings: one that soars above us, one that soaks the earth around us, and one that flies about us everywhere. When I hear this chant, I think she is teaching us something about wisdom and, in doing so, she is teaching us something about the triune God. God is above us, beyond our understanding. God is so deeply present in creation that God is present in our own earthy selves. And God is all around us, guiding us along the path of life, if we only follow the wisdom of God's lead.

Sermon Extras

Seeking Holiness

Listen to Hildegard of Bingen's "O virtus Sapientiae" (many recordings are available free online). Take a few minutes for prayer, journaling, drawing, or meditation. What does Wisdom look, smell, taste, sound, and feel like?

Worship Helps

Gathering Prayer

Divine Wisdom, encircle us, keep us upon your path. Enliven us to seek you in the heavens, upon the earth, and in all of your creation. We give you all praise, as it is right for us to do. Amen.[1]

Prayer of Illumination

[Read immediately before the reading of scripture.]

Open our minds to understand the wisdom of your Word, O God. Open our ears to hear the good news your scripture shares with us. Open our lips to declare your righteousness and open our hearts to receive the gift of your salvation in the birth of Jesus.

Benediction

May you go forth from this space enlivened by the Spirit to follow the path of Divine Wisdom, which is as present with you as it was at the beginning. Be bold to seek Divine Wisdom's presence in yourself, in your neighbor, and in all of creation. Amen.

January 10, 2021–First Sunday after the Epiphany; Baptism of the Lord

Genesis 1:1-5; Psalm 29; Acts 19:1-7; Mark 1:4-11

Will Willimon

Preaching Theme

This home of ours on earth is God's. That simple claim has two important theological implications: *The earth is not our possession* ("It's mine and I can do with it what I choose.") nor is it our achievement ("Look what a great thing I have built for myself."); *the world is God's gift.* And these theological claims come with an important ethical imperative: as receivers of God's good gift of creation *we have the responsibility to wisely and compassionately care for that gift.*

Among many of us, there is a growing recognition that humanity is taking God's well-formed earth and despoiling and destroying it back into the formless void.

I'm saying that **Genesis 1**, our first lesson for this Sunday, ought to be listened to afresh. The earth is not our possession, our achievement, or our property; the world is God's creation, God's gift, and maybe also God's assignment to us.

Thus, the Genesis command to subdue the earth means that if we are to rule, then we are to rule similarly to the way God rules us in Jesus Christ. My friend and great biblical interpreter, Ellen Davis, says that *dominion* ought to be translated not as "dominion over" but rather as "mastery among." Humanity is right to aspire to skilled mastery among creatures, including the mastery of care for all that God has created. Violence, exploitation, and abuse of what God has created is excluded from the definition of *dominion*. When Genesis moves from the creation of light and dark, plants and animals, to the creation of humanity, Genesis stresses cultivation rather than production, caregiving and stewardship rather than exploitation.

This Sunday the church focuses on Jesus's baptism, which **Mark** recounts in our Gospel lesson for today. As Jesus descends into the baptismal waters, we see a snapshot of his incarnation. As we reiterated last Sunday, Jesus is among us, as one of us, God assuming our flesh and our creaturely nature. How fitting, therefore, that Jesus's ministry opens with him standing knee deep in water, the stuff of life, performing a very earthly, human task: bathing. It is God meeting us in the stuff of creation, God appearing to us where we live, here on earth, the gift that God has given us to sustain us and to delight us.

It's a humbling thought that this world was created by God. We are God's creatures rather than the world's creators. We are created, owned, called by God rather than self-fabricated. The earth still belongs to God; the world has been entrusted to us for safekeeping rather than for exploitation.

Sermon Extras

Nurturing Creation

Some say that the Bible itself shares some responsibility for our environmental crisis. Lynn T. White (who died in 1987), a lifelong active Presbyterian layperson, began a decades-long controversy by writing an influential article that asserted that the modern world is in an environmental mess because of the creation account in **Genesis**. Scripture, according to White, put human beings at the center of creation. According to **Genesis 1:28**, God gives humanity "dominion" over the world; humanity, God's crowning achievement, is the lord of all the earth.

Does Christianity bear the blame for our present environmental crisis? Is the Genesis account of creation—which moves from God's creation to our domination—responsible for the environmental degradation?

Well, yes and no.

Much depends on how we define that word *dominion*. If giving humanity "dominion" over the earth means that the earth is our property to use as we please, then one could easily see how such an attitude would lead to some very bad results for planet earth.

On the other hand, defining *dominion* as ownership seems oddly out of place in the context of the Genesis affirmation of God's creation of the world. Today's first lesson from the first words of Genesis clearly asserts upfront that the earth is *not* our creation; the earth is God's. God giving us "dominion" does not mean God handing over God's property to us to use as if we had created it and as if we own it. That would be putting us in God's place, to dethrone God and attempt to be gods ourselves. And we all know, from another section in Genesis, the trouble that Adam and Eve got into by attempting to take the world into their hands and live as if they were not creatures but rather creators of themselves.

Furthermore, I remind you that as Christians, we define *dominion*, that is, *lordship*, not on the basis of humanity's striving for power and control, but rather on the basis of our Lord, Jesus Christ. How did Jesus exercise lordship? In today's Gospel, **Mark**'s account of Jesus's baptism, Jesus is depicted as beginning his ministry not by dashing onto the scene and taking charge of Judea but rather, Jesus is depicted as humbly submitting to John's baptism in the Jordan River by taking the form of a servant rather than that of a dominating lord, by standing in solidarity with the creatures he came to save.

We can't be lords of creation because Jesus Christ is Lord and we are not.

We should take care when reading in Genesis about human dominance. There are different ways to read Genesis 1. Lynn White was right in pointing out that Genesis places us in a human-centered universe. We are created "little less than God" (**Ps 8:5** RSV). Thinking of humanity as the center of the world can lead to bad consequences. And yet, we are *created*. As the psalmist says, "It is [God] that hath made us and not we ourselves" (**Ps 100:3** KJV).

God has created us as creatures embedded in creation, not as lords of creation.

Worship Helps

Hymns and songs related to the beauty of creation would be quite appropriate for this Sunday.

Gathering Prayer

Creator God, we give thanks this day for your overflowing, creative love. You spoke and our world came into being. The beauty of the earth, for the bounty of creation, the rising and setting of the sun, all speak to us of your goodness and grace.

As those who have been baptized, we are given the knowledge that "the earth is the Lord's." Forgive us for the times when we have abused the earth that you have given us, when we have exploited your creation as if it were ours to use as we please. Make us mindful of our duty to care for the great gift we have been given, of our responsibility to protect the planet for future generations, of our baptismal mandate to work for a more just distribution among all your children of the earth's bounty. Amen.

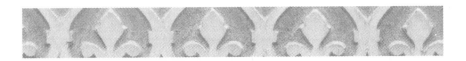

January 17, 2021–Second Sunday after the Epiphany

1 Samuel 3:1-10 (11-20); Psalm 139:1-6, 13-18; 1 Corinthians 6:12-20;
John 1:43-51

Roslyn Lee

Preaching Theme

We have a familiar call and response in the church that calls attention to the presence of God: "The Lord be with you"; the appropriate response is: "Also with you." This call and response does not work in a setting of one. And such, also, is the case with our lectionary texts as found in **1 Samuel 3:1-10** and in the Gospel of **John 1:43-51**. The awareness of God and the experience of God happens in community. Samuel and Eli. Philip and Nathanael.

It would be quite convenient for us if we could hear a loud and clear kapow! to preface the voice of God that would call us. Kapow! Bam! Smash! Boom! Wham! Then, we would have no doubt. Imagine hearing the voice of God as clear as day. We wouldn't struggle and question whether we had indeed heard it correctly. But so often God's voice is not so clear, and we may question it or even dismiss it. Samuel hears a voice in the night and is not sure what he has heard: "Samuel, Samuel." And then again, "Samuel," and then a third time. Each time Samuel answers, "I'm here," and runs to Eli. Although Samuel did not know the voice of God at the time, Eli did. By the third time, Eli realizes that the Lord is calling Samuel and instructs Samuel in what to do. Samuel benefits from Eli's knowledge and experience of God.

Much like Samuel, we too benefit from the knowledge and experiences of God that are shared with us. We also have these moments when we are unsure of what we have heard and experienced. But we are not traveling this life-journey alone. We journey along with others who, at times, help us as Eli helped Samuel. And there are times when we are to support and guide as Eli did for Samuel. Such accountability and cooperation are critical parts of our personal faith, but are also critical in the building up of the beloved community. This theme of togetherness in community can be found in today's gospel passage as well. While Jesus is on his journey into Galilee, he finds Philip and tells him to "follow me." Philip then invites Nathanael to "come and see." Philip did not keep his call and experience to himself; rather, he goes on to share them with another. Philip listens to Nathanael and helps Nathanael work through his questions until Nathanael comes to have his own experiences with Jesus.

At times, life is not obvious and we may question the sequence of events; we may even question our experiences. The encouraging truth is that we experience God in community. It's OK if we don't hear or see God moving and present in our lives at each moment. That's what accountability is for! For all those times when we were unsure of ourselves, the presence of our community confirms our experiences for us and helps us move forward in faith.

Sermon Extras

Engaging Kids

"It takes a village to raise a child." This would require the active participation of your congregation. In place of a children's sermon today, begin by splitting the congregation into smaller groups. Each group should have a child with whom faith stories of the congregation can be shared. Providing a leading question will help the "villages" share their stories. Some leading questions could be: When and where did you first experience God? Where do you see God in your life now? What led you to our church?

This is an opportunity to practice sharing our faith stories within our church community in the hope that we share these stories of God in our lives beyond the church community.

Seeking Holiness

This activity goes beyond the Sunday morning worship. Encourage your worshipping community to prayerfully write or draw accounts of their faith for them to share. Because moments of how God is experienced in an individual's life are unique, taking the time to reflect on one's faith journey can be encouraging. Have fun with it.

Worship Helps

Gathering Prayer #1

God of love and light, prepare our hearts for this hour as we listen for your voice. We desire to hear you. We desire the courage to live as though we truly know you. Encourage and enable us to live and worship as though we have no doubt. Take hold of our lives once more. In the name of the Holy One, Jesus the Christ, we pray. Amen.

Gathering Prayer #2

God of all creation, in this season of inspiration and light, be ever obvious that you are calling and leading us still. Let there be no doubt of your presence in our lives. Grant us courage to be still long enough to know you. Inspire us to live as though we truly hear you, for we desire to dwell in the assurance of your light and love today. Amen.

Response to the Word

Do you hear God calling you to this place?
Yes! We are here for we have heard the voice of God.
Will you listen and be the voice of God today to share of God's love and light?
Yes! We will listen and follow as the Spirit of God leads us to share the love and light of Christ. We will walk together on this journey, encouraging one another so that all people will come to know and experience the presence of God in their lives.

January 24, 2021–Third Sunday after the Epiphany

Jonah 3:1-5, 10; Psalm 62:5-12; 1 Corinthians 7:29-31; Mark 1:14-20

Kirsten S. Oh

Preaching Theme

In **Jonah 3**, the reluctant prophet's path finally ends at the great and sinful city of Nineveh. There Jonah proclaims, "Just forty days more" (v. 4).

"Just forty days more" can be heard differently depending on the God-image and God-concept one has and on how one perceives these words. The one who has experienced God as a harsh disciplinarian growing up in a very strict family, reinforced by similar teachings that form their God-concept may hear the words in a retributive and equally punitive way. On the other hand, the other who has experienced and learned of a compassionate God may hear the words in a restorative and grace-filled way.

Jonah knew God, yet he ran away from the call set before him. Trauma theory suggests that Jonah's reluctance and silence was a result of the oppressive powers of the Persian Empire, Nineveh being the empire's principal and capital offender.[2]

Jonah, who was in one of the oppressed groups traumatized by the atrocities done by the Ninevites, understandably wanted them extinguished and had no interest in providing the "just forty days more" warning.

So, when Jonah washed up on the shores of Nineveh and preached God's message, "just forty days more," the audience may seemingly be suspect.

This "just forty days more" message could be heard in multiple ways: (1) ignore the prophet and the message, deny the accusation, defend the state of the city as either normative or even superior to others; (2) hear it as a doomsday message and live more wildly and cruelly until the end; or (3) understand that this is a warning stemming from compassion and requiring a true act of repentance.

Just forty days more. The single story of this city as a great and evil place, which Jonah insistently held, showed cracks of inconsistencies. What about the inhabitants of the city, the local farmers, women, children, and animals? Rebecca Lindsay writes, "The vulnerable subjects of the city, those who receive rather than perpetrate its evil, are kept voiceless and unseen. Even the Nineveh described in detail by those scholars who seek to highlight the historical atrocities of the Assyrian empire would not have been so simple to pass off as a single unit."[3] These inhabitants, including the king and the high officials, wore sackcloth and ashes and repented. It's quite remarkable, perhaps even supernatural, that this message was heard around the city as a salvific message of grace and hope.

These Ninevites were not a singular, homogenous people, whose evil and wickedness were renown. Rather, all the inhabitants of the city—the voiceless and unseen ones, the ones who generated evil for which the city gained renown, and those who were in the middle of these spectrums—got to experience God, whom Jonah knew: "a merciful and compassionate God, very patient, full of faithful love, and willing not to destroy" (**Jonah 4:2**). The untruth of the empire's, and of the city's, label was revealed when confronted with the powerful message, "just forty days more," a message from a God who was unwilling to destroy.

Sermon Extras

Engaging Kids

Sometimes we like to place groups of people into boxes that we can label and categorize because we may not know them well, or we may not like the ways in which they are different. In the story of **Jonah**, we learn that Jonah had placed an entire great city into a large box of stereotypes and did not want to help them with God's call for repentance and restoration. He thought that they were bad and evil people.

Have you ever been categorized by other people? Or have you ever categorized others? If so, what might those categorizations be? (Note: have ready-made boxes with labels that you can write down categorizations, such as good, bad, friendly, mean, bully, and so on that the children may suggest when prompted.)

In the story today, we read about God's prophet who labels a whole city of people into one category and refuses to give them God's message of love. However, we know that labels are for boxes and jars, not for people.

Through Jonah, God teaches us that God loves all of God's created beings and knows that none of us fit under one label. A whole group of people cannot be broadly categorized into either good or bad. In fact, even an individual with the reputation of being bad, and who may have even earned that reputation, is more than that label. That's why today's biblical reading teaches us that *all* the people in the city repented—the good, the bad, and the ugly. That is because the God that you and I believe in is "a merciful and compassionate God, very patient, full of faithful love, and willing not to destroy" (**Jonah 4:2**).

Worship Helps

Gathering Prayer

O God,
We thank you as we continuously celebrate the incarnation of God in Jesus Christ and the revelation of who you really are to both the Jews and the Gentiles.

Shape, form, and reform our images of you that we may understand the true picture of who you are. Reveal to us your nature and character that we may hear more clearly, see more brightly, and understand more deeply your love.

We ask humbly that you would deepen our understanding so that we may be an extension of you in our families, neighbors, country, and the world. Amen.

Call to Worship (Based on Psalm 62:5-12)

Come, find rest in God only.
Because my hope comes from God.
All you people: trust in him at all times! Pour out your hearts before him!
God is our refuge, our rock, our salvation, and our stronghold!—We will not be shaken.
ALL: Faithful love comes from you, our God. Amen

Sending Forth

As we go out from this place of worship, may the merciful and compassionate God, very patient, full of faithful love, and willing not to destroy, teach us to open wide our arms to the world that God has created. Live into the image of God, who loves while we were yet unrepentant, and calls us to love all the created beings so that we may be connected to God and with one another. Amen.

January 31, 2021–Fourth Sunday after the Epiphany

Deuteronomy 18:15-20; Psalm 111; 1 Corinthians 8:1-13; Mark 1:21-28

Karyn L. Wiseman

Preaching Theme

The Gospel this week tells one of the many healing stories from **Mark**. The author of this Gospel told the well-known story of Jesus to his community in a new way. This is the shortest of the four Gospels and it has the least connection to the stories we know best about Jesus's life. There are no accounts of the good Samaritan, the story of Mary and Martha, the Samaritan woman at the well, the prodigal son, or other stories that influence how we "know" Jesus. However, there are some powerful images in Mark—the feeding of the five thousand, the healing of the deaf and mute man, the rich young ruler, and others.[4]

In this text we see Jesus confronting an impure spirit that has inhabited a man. Jesus is teaching in the synagogue when he encounters this spirit and Jesus's response is to call the spirit out. This is a moment in which we see all of who Jesus is—rabbi, teacher, prophet, healer, and divine son of God. It's the kind of moment that reminds us how profoundly Jesus impacted the lives of those he interacted with at that time and, as a result, how these stories can impact our lives today. He could have walked away when the man approached him, but he chose to stay and do something about the situation. This is a witness to how we are called to live, to be present with those in need, to respond to their needs as we are able, and to proclaim the power of God through Jesus Christ to others. Through this story, Jesus's notoriety begins to spread. While this is an account of Jesus's great power over an unclean spirit, it is also a look at Jesus's humanity. Jesus hears the need and responds.

Healing stories in the biblical text can cause significant issues for both preachers and listeners. Questions may arise, such as: Why is this person healed when others are not? Why does this family get its wish while so many other families suffer without interventions? Preaching about healing means avoiding false promises, encourages us to speak the truth about disease and illness, and makes us seek answers. Trying to provide all of these in your sermon can bring false hope and may take advantage of your listeners' vulnerability. The realities of this text provide us with a caution to consider while preaching; the text also shows us the authoritative power and might of Jesus to impact lives. These are the stories that have the potential to make our lives more hope-filled. Tap into these stories to help your folks feel the presence of a healing and loving savior.

While Mark can drive me crazy at times with the misunderstandings, secrets, and the disciples' failure to comprehend what was happening around them, this story clearly shows who Jesus is and the power he has at his disposal. The power of Mark as a sparse story, which in its earliest version did not even include the Resurrection, means that his Gospel shows us a Jesus who is active. Mark portrays Jesus teaching and healing as he relates to the suffering of humanity around him. The action starts early and continues throughout this Gospel account of Jesus's life. This story is one of those active moments that teaches us to respond to the needs of those around us.

Sermon Extras

Engaging Kids

Children often have issues with healing stories. Create an opportunity to talk about a pet or a friend who has gone to the vet or the hospital. You can ask what was scary about that time and ask them what helped them feel better. You can share a story about a pet that had a medical issue and got help. I have taken bandages or a kid's doctor kit with me for these types of lessons. Depending on your context and the kids' ages, you can also share the story with either more or fewer details. Having easy answers is not the way to go; instead, help children know that sometimes the vet or doctor can help and sometimes they can't. God is with us no matter what.

We can do something concrete to help by interacting in personal and profound ways with those who suffer. Doing so can spark your community of faith to be more connected to their physical surroundings. There are many ways to act for the benefit of your community, such as knitting prayer shawls or lap rugs for those who are experiencing health crises, donating stuffed animals to local police officers to give to children whom they encounter in their daily shifts, or volunteering to be present with those who are dealing with grief or loss. Doing something tangible for your community can lessen the feelings of helplessness that often accompany these moments.

Worship Helps

Gathering Prayer

Holy One, speak to us. Lead us to listen when you speak. Help us to close our mouths to receive your word more fully. Help us to open our ears to hear your word this day and into the future. Help us to open our hearts to care for the concerns of others and to respond with love and grace to those in need. Amen.

Call to Worship

We come into this place to hear the word sung, read, and proclaimed.
We come together to be the people of God in worship.
We stay to be part of a community of caring and grace.
We stay to find hope in the midst of hopelessness and pain.
We go back into the world to be the hands and feet of Christ for others.
We go out to share the news of our Savior and Lord with all. Amen and amen.

Offertory Invitation

God of love and grace, we bring our gifts to this altar to bring hope and healing in all the ways we can. We bring our bodies as living offerings to provide presence and support to those in need. We bring our prayers and voices to provide voice and witness for those who cannot speak. We bring our purpose and faithfulness to proclaim the power of Jesus in our lives. Bless these, our offerings, and make them be for the world what it needs in times of despair. Amen.

February 7, 2021—Fifth Sunday after the Epiphany

Isaiah 40:21-31; Psalm 147:1-11, 20c; 1 Corinthians 9:16-23; Mark 1:29-39

Grace S. Pak

Focusing Prayer

Lord, open my eyes so that I can see all your people.
Open my heart so that I can embrace all your people.
Open my life so that I can be the good news of Jesus Christ to all your people. Amen.

Preaching Theme

We are all passionate about something. What are you passionate about? Paul is passionate about the gospel of Jesus Christ; all his activities center on making the gospel known to all people and his writings are saturated with his passion. In fact, his lifestyle is all about giving witness to the love of Jesus Christ. This pericope from **1 Corinthians** begins with Paul explaining what ministry means to him. When ministry is going well, it is fun. When the going gets tough, he doesn't give up, but continues because sharing the gospel is his calling. He is compelled to do it and he is willing to give everything for the advancement of the gospel.

Paul is passionate for the good news of Christ and is resolved to share it with all people, regardless of their theological stance, value system, racial and cultural background, or whatever other distinctions there may be. Paul shares insights about how to share the gospel with "others," whether they are like him or different.

To start, Paul sees people as *who* they are and *where* they are and accepts them *as* they are. Paul is willing to meet people where they are and connect with them. Paul is intentional about connecting with everyone as they are rather than waiting for them to be like him or demanding that they meet certain criteria. Jesus met him as he was on the road to Damascus, on his way toward violence against the believers of Christ. If Jesus waited until Paul's practice and heart were changed, Paul might have never connected with Christ. Thus, Paul says, "I act like a Jew to the Jews...I act like I'm under the Law to those under the Law...I act like I'm outside the Law to those who are outside the Law . . . I act weak to the weak" (1 Cor 9:20-22). Diversity is the reality of our world. Inclusion is imperative. It is God's great mandate for the church.

Paul then says, "I have become all things to all people," to reach and connect with as many people as possible (9:22). What Paul describes is having empathy, the ability to understand and share another's feelings or having the willingness to put oneself in another's shoes. Eugene Peterson translates the text appropriately in *The Message*: "I didn't take on their way of life. I kept my bearings in Christ—but I entered their world and tried to experience things from their point of view" (9:19-23). For Paul to go from having a set of beliefs, customs, and culture specific to his context to "becom[ing] all things to all people" means he had to put in extra effort and work to share in others' experiences and to understand "others" who are different from him in many aspects. Empathy is hard work. To understand and share others' experiences and their points of view means one has to set aside one's own familiar thoughts and perceptions to make room for new encounters and understanding others. One has to suspend judgment and open oneself up to diverse ways of seeing and experiencing the world. For Paul, all of this hard work is worth it because empathy creates the space necessary for getting to know others and to build relationships; empathy opens the portal to love as Jesus loved and to sharing the gospel. No one can connect with "others" unless there is a genuine sharing of feelings and a mutual understanding of each other's experiences.

But merely having a heart open to accepting others as they are and the empathy to understand and share others' perspectives are not sufficient for Paul. Paul undergirded these interactions with extreme servant leadership: "I make myself a slave to all people" (9:19). Paul's choice of the word *slave* encapsulates a profound servanthood and humility. The focus is solely on the other and their needs, not on the one who serves. This means giving of oneself without any recognition or restitution.

What would it look like for the church to practice extreme servant leadership in its surrounding community? What kind of effect would it have on connecting others with Jesus?

Paul's passion is Jesus; his desire is to be a partner of the gospel. Why? Because this is what God has done for him and for each of us. God came to us and loved us first before we knew God (**1 John 4:19**). In Christ, God comes and embraces us *where* we are and *as* we are through Christ coming down to our level and accepting us as sinners. Jesus showed his love for us by giving up his life for us. For Paul, to be "a partner with the gospel" means to do for others what God has done for him. Who is missing at the Lord's Table in your church? Who is God nudging you to reach out to; to empathize with; to serve and to invite to partner with in the gospel?

Sermon Extras

Doing Justice

Organize a community walk-around. Encourage congregation members to walk around the town, either as a group or individually, and pay attention to the following questions:

Who is invisible in your community?

Who are the people on the other side of the tracks, town, river, and so on?

Where are they from? Learn about them, their joys, difficulties, and so on.

In what ways can the church connect with them and show Jesus's love?

Share your findings with others and seek ways to connect with them and love them, just as Jesus has loved you.

Worship Helps

Invocation

O God, you have created us as your people and called us to partner with you in spreading the good news of Jesus Christ to the ends of the earth so that all your people can be in relationship with you and with each other. May the Holy Spirit fill us with passion and enthusiasm for the gospel so that we can serve and love with all that we are and with all that we have. We pray in the name of Jesus, our example and savior. Amen.

Prayer of Repentance

O God, you have created us in your image and called us to partner with you to spread the good news to all your people. Too often, we have defined "all your people" to be those who are like us in the way we look, speak, and live. We have shied away from going across boundaries to those who are different and we have withheld your love. We have judged those who are different according to our standards, not knowing their circumstances. Forgive us, O God. Fill our hearts with your love and compassion for others. Give us courage to step out of our comfort zones and reach out with the love of Jesus Christ so that we can partner with you in enlarging your Kin-dom here on earth. We pray in Jesus's name, our example and savior. Amen.

Sending Forth

As we leave this place, may you go with your eyes wide open to see those who are different and invisible. May you go with your ears trained to hear different languages and sounds. May you go with your hearts and arms spread open to embrace those who are different, for they are God's children and your brothers and sisters. And in your openness, may God's love be experienced by all who are in your path. Amen.

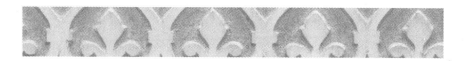

February 14, 2021– Transfiguration Sunday

2 Kings 2:1-12; Psalm 50:1-6; 2 Corinthians 4:3-6; Mark 9:2-9

Javier A. Viera

Preaching Theme

On a day in the secular calendar that we've come to associate with love and all things romantic, the church's calendar and scriptures remind us that true love is costly, true love is demanding, and that true love is transformative. The gospel for today tells of Jesus going on a brief pilgrimage with three of his most trusted friends. They climb a high mountain for a time of quiet, retreat, and anticipation of God's powerful presence among them. The setting alone suggests that something profound is about to happen and, indeed, it does.

Peter, James, and John witness the collapsing of time and space on that mountainside, when God makes known, through Moses, Elijah, and Jesus, how God has been at work throughout human history and time. In an unprecedented display of divine power and presence, Jesus is joined by the great liberator, Moses, and the great prophet, Elijah—two of ancient Israel's brightest and greatest lights—to reveal the fullness of God in a peasant carpenter of Nazareth. What is clear to both the disciples and to Mark's readers is that Jesus is God's fullness, God's real presence, and God's way forward in the world.

Rather than find comfort and relief in this theophany, Peter seems troubled, or at least unsure of what to do with this. He knows it's an important moment, an important indicator of what is to come, but he seems unsure of what to do with this new, deeper knowledge. To understand Peter's reaction to the mountaintop theophany, it's important to put it into the larger context of what **Mark** is unfolding at this point in his Gospel. Today's reading began with the phrase, "Six days later . . . ," which should lead one to ask what had previously transpired that Mark is connecting to this moment. Six days prior, after having inexplicably fed four thousand people, after having taken on the religious establishment, after having restored a blind man's sight, and after having been declared by Peter that he was the Messiah, Jesus gathered a crowd and began to teach them that more difficult days were ahead, for him and for all who followed him. He would suffer and be killed, and many of them would have to make peace with similar fates if they were to take his teachings seriously and to follow him fully. Peter couldn't accept this; he challenged and corrected Jesus, not allowing for a model of leadership or a model of the messiah that did not overcome those who opposed him through power and might. Jesus rebuked Peter's correction, saying to him chillingly, "Get behind me, Satan, for you have your own concerns, and not the concerns of God in mind" (**Matt 16:23**, paraphrased). This is what took place six days prior and now God's fullness is being revealed to Peter and the others on the mountain.

Peter again seems to miss the point. He assumes that Jesus is being revealed as the same kind of leader as Moses, the great liberator, and Elijah, the great prophet, who were revered and constantly invoked by all their people throughout the ages. But given what Jesus had taught six days earlier, which Peter was reluctant to accept, it seems God is revealing something else here. Building three monuments honoring the great men of history was hardly a response appropriate to the moment and the content of what had just been revealed. God, in Jesus, is doing something new; God is doing something radically different from what had been required of leaders in the past. Instead, Moses and Elijah are present to ostensibly give their blessing to the new direction of God's movement Jesus embodies and reveals. But Peter is scandalized by what Jesus reveals; he is hesitant to follow someone who is not prepared to conquer by might and by sword. The way of sacrifice, of peace, of selfless love doesn't instinctively resonate with his ambitions or visions for how to bring about radical change. Seeming to capture Peter's attitude or outlook, in the epistle lesson for this day, the apostle Paul says, "The god of this world has blinded the minds of the unbelievers, to keep them from seeing the light of the gospel of the glory of Christ, who is the image of God" (**2 Cor 4:4** NRSV). We often mistakenly read this as a statement against non-Christians, yet Paul here is referencing those who cannot accept or hear the very difficult message of Jesus as the embodiment of the God of peace and the God of love. The "god of this world" is the violence we depend on and look to in order to resolve our differences, and this violent god is manifest in our political structures, economic systems, and social orders that perpetuate ways of being that do not foster reconciliation and collective thriving.

Yet on that mountainside, Jesus quietly insists that monuments and honors are not what he is after. What he wants Peter, James, and John to understand is that in the radiant light they have just witnessed, they are seeing God, they are seeing that God intends this way of sacrifice, peace, and selfless love to be the way forward, and that reality is what Moses and Elijah bless. The way of domination, of scapegoating, of the sword has passed and the people of God must embody a new way forward. That is what God in Jesus reveals, both to them and to us. In their own leadership challenges, Moses killed a man in a moment of passionate defense and Elijah ordered that those he perceived as enemies of God be slaughtered. On that mountaintop, God declares that in Jesus things will be different and that those who follow him and follow the ways of God will also have to be different. God makes this abundantly clear in one simple, spoken statement: "This is my Son, the Beloved; listen to him" (Mark 9:7 NRSV). That's the task before us, and the message we must proclaim.

Sermon Extras

Engaging Kids

In some ways, children understand the difficulty of this lesson better than most adults. This might be a good opportunity to engage children in a conversation about who they understand God to be, and how they perceive God to be at work and present in the world. Be open to their surprising insights, but also be sure to use this story's rich imagery to teach them that, in Jesus, God has chosen to be fully known and that following Jesus's ways—his kindness, his peacefulness, and his loving gentleness—is how God calls us to live in the world and to resolve the inevitable challenges that present themselves to us each day.

Worship Helps

Gathering Prayer

Blessed are you, Lord God of all creation, for you have revealed to us your glory, your splendor, and your goodness. In Christ, you give yourself to us, not only as an act of selfless love, but also as an example of who and what we might become. Continue to reveal yourself to us in your fullness, even as we strive to grow into your likeness that we may come to embody the grandeur and the costliness of your love and mercy in a violent and fractured world. Amen.

Benediction

My sisters, brothers, and siblings in Christ, our worship never ends; it must be lived. Go forth from this place to be the visible, tangible love of God in a fractured and troubled world. And as you do so, know that the peace of Christ dwells within you and works through you to bring all of creation into the fullness of God. Amen.

February 17, 2021– Ash Wednesday

Joel 2:1-2, 12-17 or Isaiah 58:1-12; Psalm 51:1-17; 2 Corinthians 5:20b–6:10; Matthew 6:1-6, 16-21

Laurie K. Zelman

Preaching Theme

The lectionary scriptures for Ash Wednesday call in different ways for Christians to undertake some practice that will lead to a deeper relationship with the divine. The contrast and complement of the verses from **Matthew** and the passage from **Joel** are especially striking; one contains Jesus's instruction for solitary prayer and the other describes a faith community fasting together.

Many people, perhaps younger people especially, express fear and pessimism about the future. They are concerned that changes the planet is undergoing have been set in motion and are already unstoppable and that, in short, the earth is doomed to ecological tragedy. The Joel passage expresses a kindred fear, but it also expresses hope that the dark future portrayed in the passage that surrounds the lectionary excerpt might yet be averted, if the people turn back to God. What is called for is a fast; Joel calls out to gather everyone—from the elders to the infants to the young adults—to start a committed life together and to fast as a way of praying for the impending disaster to be averted.

Now, humanity has perspectives like it has never had before. We have seen the smallness of the earth from space, we can feel humanity in its many expressions, and humanity's vision is powered by a worldwide connection. If we care to look, we can *see* the marks of voracious, careless consumption and disposal in God's world. The meaning of fasting may expand to encompass this new awareness.

The Matthew passage carries Jesus's instruction about how to pray and how not to pray. We are cautioned by Jesus not to pray like hypocrites. The word *hypocrite* comes from the Greek word *hypokrites*, meaning actor. In Greece's classical era, actors performed in festivals that honored the god Dionysus. These actors held masks up in front of their faces; some masks were comic and were shaped to mimic the extremes of human emotion; other masks were tragic and portrayed images of Greek heroes and gods. Actors could play many roles in a single play, transforming themselves into different characters using the masks.

One way we can respond to Jesus's admonition is to reflect on the truth that prayer is not a performance for others' benefit or to impress God. When we pray, we should not portray someone other than who we are. Instead, we are invited to open ourselves up. This act, which allows the Holy Spirit to search and know our most private selves, can be done in a room full of worshipers or in solitude. The essence of the act is the transformation that can occur when we drop the masks, for in letting God look, know, judge, and love us, we can both know more about what and who we are and begin to become more fully what God intends us to be.

Sermon Extras

Seeking Holiness

Ash Wednesday and Lent can be times when faith can be enriched by taking on devotional practices.

Fasting: Traditionally, many give up a favorite food or one meal per week and then some donate the money saved from abstaining from these foods or meals to assist others. But fasting can take many forms: giving up the use of plastic bags in the supermarket, abstaining from screen time, walking to do errands instead of driving, or resetting the thermostat to save energy. One might even undertake the mental discipline of giving up negative patterns of thinking and replacing those thoughts with words that express God's providence and leading. One example would be giving up the thought "I hate this job" and countering it with the thought "God gave me this job for a reason."

Prayer: Walking a prayer labyrinth expresses the inward and outward movement that is part of the prayer journey. One of many possible formats might be to focus on what one needs to put down or give up as one walks to the center of the labyrinth. Then, on the journey outward from the labyrinth's center, one could allow the Holy Spirit to fill the empty places resulting from giving other things up. Labyrinths can be found in many communities, or a temporary labyrinth could be constructed by putting tape on the floor, by mowing a pattern in grass, or a small labyrinth could be printed out and "walked" by tracing it with a finger.

Engaging Kids

On a Sunday or two leading up to Lent, you can provide children and youths with papers containing a picture of a cross and ask them to write suggestions for which disciplines they could "take up" during Lent. These suggestions might include the traditional ones, such as "give up sweets," but they could also include fasts such as "don't take plastic straws," "bring your own shopping bags," or "turn your phone off every day for a set time"; or they could include disciplines such as "visit a homebound individual," "pray for victims of human trafficking," or "donate peanut butter and tuna to the food pantry." These written suggestions, along with blank paper for writing down different options, could be incorporated into an Ash Wednesday service and offered again on Sunday for congregants to make a selection and adopt them as a practice during Lent, either as individuals or as families.

Worship Helps

Gathering Prayer

Holy one, this day we are stepping into the journey of Lent, a path that leads us through ends and on into new beginnings, as we walk with Christ to the cross and beyond to the Resurrection. The journey leads outward to our neighbors, our congregation, the crowd in the streets, and inward toward the center of our prayers and the center of our hearts. Help us, God, to be aware of your leading, to follow in faith the journey you have set before us. Amen.

Call to Worship

The path lies before us.
Let us set our feet upon the path.
In the distance we hear a cheering crowd.
Beyond, we see the dark shadow of the cross.
Grant us courage, O God,
Send your Spirit to walk beside us.

Prayer of Repentance

We have fallen short, O God. When you ask us to strive for awareness, we settle for slogans. When our hearts should be breaking, we turn away. When our eyes should overflow with tears, we turn to distractions. When you ask us to reach out to our neighbors, we retreat to comfortable places. When you ask us to be stewards, we relapse into careless consumption. Forgive us, merciful God, do not turn away from us. Cleanse us, create in us clean hearts. Put a new and right spirit within us. Amen.

February 21, 2021–First Sunday in Lent

Genesis 9:8-17; Psalm 25:1-10; 1 Peter 3:18-22; Mark 1:9-15

Sudarshana Devadhar

Preaching Theme

A mentor of mine once told me that people in the pews are more apt to hear the joyful message of the good news and respond to the formidable call to faithful obedience to the gospel during two seasons of the church year: Lent and Advent. Though one may challenge this assumption, I have found it to be true in my experience as a pastor. With that challenge and opportunity in mind, I offer my thoughts and possibilities for preaching on the gospel text for the first Sunday in Lent.

First, **Mark** says that as soon as Jesus was baptized, "there was a voice from heaven: 'You are my Son, whom I dearly love; in you I find happiness'" (Mark 1:11). The preacher may encourage listeners to relate their own baptism to Jesus's baptism and to ponder the proposition that God's love for them is indistinguishable from God's love for Jesus. Each and every one of us is God's beloved child, just as Jesus is God's beloved. Preaching this Sunday's Gospel text may provide a teaching moment for congregations to reflect on the fact that God loved Jesus before he was baptized! In the same way, God loves every person before he or she is baptized. God's love extends to all whom God has made; this was true from the beginning and will be true forever. In the sacrament of baptism, we affirm the Creator's amazing love and grace for all of God's people and that all are given power through the Spirit to love what God loves.

Second, as a pastor, you have undoubtedly met parents who want to have their children baptized to ensure "that nothing will happen to them." It is as if the God who created them would withhold love, blessing, and life from their child if he or she were not baptized; it is as if they believe that baptism would keep their children safe from all harm. All of us need to be reminded again and again that baptism is not a sentimental ceremony or a kind of vaccination to shield the baptized from trouble. Quite the contrary! Our baptism, like Jesus's baptism, initiates and inaugurates us into a life of suffering with Christ (that ultimately and paradoxically leads to the fullness of life). Through baptism we come to know ourselves as God's beloved who find abundant life through dying and rising with Christ over and over again. Our baptism drives us into the wilderness where we are sure to encounter the wild beasts of the twenty-first century: beasts of power, beasts of control, and beasts of all the "isms." Baptism is a call to resist evil in whatever form it presents itself—in ourselves and in others—in its myriad manifestations: racism, sexism, arrogance, homophobia, xenophobia, greed, anti-Semitism, narcissism, poverty, oppression, abuse of power, abdication of power, apathy, and so on.

Third, listeners can be reminded that, just as God sent angels to care for Jesus in the wilderness, so God will send angels to care for us when we encounter such powers and principalities in our daily lives. As a preacher, you might share a story about how you were ministered to in your own life when you encountered modern-day beasts or faced evil temptations.

Sermon Extras

Seeking Holiness

This text offers an opportunity for preachers to share stories of modern-day saints who have experienced the wilderness, confronted "wild animals," resisted evil and temptation, or engaged principalities and powers, and yet were cared for by God's angels. The list might include stories about people, such as bishops Leontine Kelly and Dale White, the Rev. Dr. Martin Luther King Jr., Dietrich Bonhoeffer, Dr. Ida Scudder, or the saints Oscar Romero and Mother Teresa. It might also recall the story of another servant of God who is known only to a few. Such stories can inspire, awaken, and encourage listeners to reflect on the Spirit's call in their own lives to fulfill the commitments made at their baptism and to employ the gifts that the Spirit has bestowed on them for the common good.

Worship Helps

Gathering Prayer

God of grace, whose Spirit descended like a dove upon Jesus at his baptism; whose voice spoke from the heavens and called him "beloved"; whose Spirit immediately drove him into the wilderness for forty days where he was tempted by Satan and lived among wild animals: help us comprehend with our whole selves that your Spirit has been poured out upon us, that we are your beloved children, and that you send us into the wildernesses of this world where we, too, are tempted by evil and confronted by the beasts of the twenty-first century. Give us courage to persevere and grant us faith to believe that we can count upon your angels to be our hosts. We pray through Christ, who lives and reigns with you and the Holy Spirit, one God, forever and ever. Amen.

Call to Worship (Based on Psalm 25:4-6)

Make your ways known to me, Lord;
Teach me your paths.
Lead me in your truth; teach it to me.
Because you are the God who saves me,
I put my hope in you all day long.
Lord, remember your compassion and faithful love;
they are forever.

Benediction

Beloved of God,
Go to your neighbor in peace.
Go into the wildernesses where God sends you.
Go in the knowledge that, when you encounter trials and temptations,
God's angels will care for you.
Go forth in the name of the Father, the Son, and the Holy Spirit. Amen.

February 28, 2021–Second Sunday in Lent

Genesis 17:1-7, 15-16; Psalm 22:23-31; Romans 4:13-25; Mark 8:31-38 or Mark 9:2-9

Tanya Linn Bennett

Preaching Theme

Of course, this passage from the eighth chapter of the Gospel of **Mark** is a familiar one to us. But no matter how often I hear it, I am fraught with an overwhelming dismay, even fear—not only at Jesus's proclamation that we must lose ourselves, bearing our crosses, to find new life, but also at Jesus's rebuke of Peter and the use of the term "Satan" when addressing Peter after Peter's reaction to the account of Jesus's death and resurrection. But this next statement that Jesus makes always helps me come back to this text: "You are not thinking God's thoughts but human thoughts" (Mark 8:33).

Throughout his ministry, Jesus reminded the disciples that they must leave everything behind if they were to follow him. Even as he calls them away from their fishing nets, he reminds them that they must leave their "dead" behind. He claims in **Matthew 10** that he did not come to bring peace but a sword, a sword that will divide families and sever friend from friend, neighbor from neighbor. It is not only an incisive message of the cost of discipleship but also of the glory of life lived in God's thoughts and the liberation from human ways and thoughts that oppress, judge, separate, and marginalize.

The writer of Matthew then expands the message. It is no longer only for the twelve disciples, but for an entire crowd that gathers: "All who want to come after me must say no to themselves, take up their cross and follow me" (**Matt 16:24**). Matthew's ongoing concern is whether the Jewish people, along with nonbelievers, would hear Jesus's call to new life—a call for the masses, not confined to the twelve disciples. No wonder Jesus must set Peter straight before he can address a broader audience. If his own selected band of travelers can't get it right, how could he possibly convince those who have not had the experience of witnessing Jesus in action? This Satan of human thought must be excised from the message if there is any hope to convince those who are imprisoned by human thought that there is a different way, a better way, a more holy way.

As we consider our human status during the reflective time of Lent, what is it that we must leave behind in order to move forward in discipleship? Can we identify the specific human concerns that keep us from freedom in the love and hope of Christ Jesus? What would be possible if we could leave those human concerns behind and walk in liberation into the light of resurrection?

If we imagine ourselves as the risen ones, the ones that rise up over and above the human concerns that distract us, mislead us, and overwhelm us, then we are empowered to be God's beloved ones who are created for a world that desperately needs us to pay attention. To pay attention not to what is, but to what could become if only we were to make room for it. But we must clear away a space; we must be willing and ready to let go of what we know now for what we can't even yet dream. That is God's offer to us, especially in the season of Lent.

Sermon Extras

Seeking Holiness

Offer an intentional time during the worship experience for people to reflect in silence or with musical accompaniment. During this time of reflection, invite people to identify one human concern that they will set aside during Lent and replace with a personal prayer for greater focus on God's dream for them. Offer them this time to actually write this three- to four-line prayer, which they can carry with them throughout this season and maybe beyond Easter as a touchstone reminding them of Jesus's call to "lose ourselves" in order to gain new life.

Worship Helps

Gathering Prayer

To find you, Jesus, we must lose ourselves. We don't often comprehend what this means. We are frightened when we hear you say this hard thing. Pour into us your courage, your faithfulness, and your hope that losing ourselves leads us into the resurrection path. Amen.

Call to Worship (Based on Psalm 22)

We offer praise in the great congregation
because of you.
ALL: Let all those who are suffering eat and be full!
Let all who seek the LORD praise him!
ALL: Every part of the earth
will remember and come back to God;
every family among all the nations will worship.
   Let us praise God's holy name!

March 7, 2021–Third Sunday in Lent

Exodus 20:1-17; Psalm 19; 1 Corinthians 1:18-25; John 2:13-22

Roslyn Lee

Preaching Theme

Priorities. During the season of Lent, we give things up in an effort to prioritize our lives once again by decluttering and focusing on that which we should be more grateful for. In our Gospel text, Jesus was cleaning up house of the things and the people cluttering it and making it into something other than a place of worship as it was intended. At the time, the things needed for worship were no longer personal. People had stopped bringing cows, sheep, and pigeons, which they had raised at home and with care because there was a danger of their livestock dying on the long journey to Jerusalem. At first, to ensure that they made it to Jerusalem with a living cow, sheep, or goat for sacrifice, people would bring with them two or even three animals, rather than just one. It was a long and difficult journey to the place of worship and, with livestock, the economic loss endured for Passover could be pretty significant.

It made sense, then, to the devoted worshipper to provide livestock to all worshippers in case someone's pigeon (or cow or sheep) didn't survive the journey to the temple. It would be nice to think that this sense of devotion to worship and taking care of and providing for the least of these was in the minds of those who set up shop near the temples. But this wasn't the case...Those who set up shop were people who saw a need from which they could profit. Savvy business-minded farmers set up stands with grain to be sold for grain offerings and livestock for sacrifices. As a result, people no longer needed to take such a big risk. They could sell a cow at home and bring the money with them to buy a cow at the temple. What was once a side market eventually took over the temple of God.

People had started cutting corners and were looking for easier ways to sacrifice; by doing so, they had lost the essence of value in the ritual acts of sacrifice. This continues to happen in our world today. I imagine that Jesus knew the culture and the need for animals to sacrifice. I imagine Jesus knew that the market by the temple could have begun as a service but turned into an exploitation of the people of God—and especially of the house of God. The Jews who had witnessed Jesus overturning the tables and upsetting sales questioned Jesus: "By what authority are you doing these things?" Jesus answered, "Destroy this temple and in three days I'll raise it up" (**John 2:18-19**). This is a difficult thing to imagine, let alone comprehend, for the Jews who were challenging Jesus because the temple in question had been under construction for forty-six years! It took forty-six years to build up this place of worship; how could Jesus build it up again in only three days?

Jesus and the Jews were talking about two different things; their priorities were different. The Jews were referring to the upset of the temple's daily functions. It was profitable for the temple to have the moneychangers and the farmers selling their goods. Meanwhile, Jesus was referring to the hearts of the people. Jesus, in overturning the tables and making a whip out of cords, had called out a brokenness in the temple which the people had grown comfortable with. Jesus called attention to the manner in which people had been approaching worship and furthering their relationship and dependence on God. In this passage, they were no longer praying and seeking God's guidance to provide safe travel for them and their livestock to and from Jerusalem. They had mistakenly assumed that they made it to the temple to worship and sacrifice because they had worked hard and provided for themselves. When they cut costs and cut out the risk of losing their livestock, they also cut out their sense of urgency and care for the journey. When the sacrifice did take place, they didn't see the cow they had fed, washed, and cared for over the years. Rather, their sacrifice was bought. They were not giving up something of value to them in making the sacrifice because there was no personal attachment; it had become merely a transaction, a transaction with the moneychanger or a transaction with the farmer who sold the livestock. And now a transaction with God. They had upheld their part of the covenant; they had taken the journey, just like their ancestors before them had done. They had sacrificed, just like their ancestors before them had done. It had become a sacrifice merely to appease God, or maybe something done out of habit. Jesus calls out the moneychangers and those who sell sacrifices...but further, he calls out everyone for their manner of worship. The covenant between God and God's forgetful people was at stake.

Perhaps we need to reexamine our priorities to be sure that God is once again at the center of our lives. Where have we cut corners in our discipleship? In our worship? In our relationship with God?

Sermon Extras

Engaging Kids

This is an opportunity to teach children about priorities. What's most important and why? How do we prioritize our ministry with our children, both in and out of the church? Give the children an opportunity to share what is the most important part of the Sunday worship experience for them and why. Be specific in asking for suggestions to improve the church experience; you may be surprised what the children of your church share with you.

Doing Justice

Are there areas of ministry or mission that no longer serve their purpose but have become activities done simply because they've always been done? Invite your congregation to prioritize missions and ministries of the church, activity by activity, to focus once again on the making of disciples and the building up of the beloved community. Prioritize. Be honest in this examination. Name the people who may have been wronged, both intentionally and unintentionally. Work to reconcile relationships as activities that no longer serve their intended purpose are allowed to end.

Worship Helps

Gathering Prayer

God of all seasons, help us to refocus our attention on you and the ways in which you build up your beloved community. Overturn our lives and reorder them so that we may be in sync with you. In Christ we pray. Amen.

Prayer of Repentance

God of forgiveness, we have not been faithful in keeping you at the center of our lives. We blame our schedules, our situations, and our lack of resources. We are quick to place blame on others rather than on ourselves as we slowly pushed you off to the side. Forgive us as we turn back to you and reorder our lives to put you first. Remind us and encourage us of your love and grace so that we can uphold our promises to be your faithful people. In Christ we pray. Amen.

March 14, 2021–Fourth Sunday in Lent

Numbers 21:4-9; Psalm 107:1-3, 17-22; Ephesians 2:1-10; John 3:14-21

Drew A. Dyson

Preaching Theme

"No condemnation, no place for fear / God's invitation to everyone here."[1] I remember singing the words of this song, which were written by my friend Steve Mugglin, when I was a young adult struggling to come to terms with my place in the world. Condemnation was what I knew. Fear I understood. Unconditional love...not so much. My religious construct was based on measuring my worth, which was based on my ability to follow the rules. God's role was to judge my worth. More often than not, I simply did not measure up.

The Pharisee Nicodemus similarly understood his faith in terms of his ability to follow the rules. His faith was genuine, rooted in a strong desire to follow God. The rules of the pharisaic sect, so often criticized, were authentic responses to faith and holy living. Jesus's response to Nicodemus, however, reframes holiness as a loving response to God's act of grace, rather than as a religious adherence rooted in the fear of condemnation.

Judgment and condemnation are human constructs rooted in fear. Grace is the gift of God rooted in unconditional love. Too often, at least in my own experience, I prefer the former. Or, at least I understand it better. Grace, as the writer of Ephesians reminds us, is God's gift of salvation in Jesus Christ, offered to us in love, even in the midst of our own human frailty.

Human nature is the choice to live in fear—to live under the scepter of condemnation. It is a choice to live under the safe cover of darkness. Yet, like Nicodemus, we approach in the dark and encounter the light: "God did not send the Son into the world to condemn the world, but in order that the world might be saved through him" (**John 3:17** NRSV).

Sermon Extras

Seeking Holiness

This sermon is an opportunity for faith-sharing, inviting testimonies offered by folks who have experienced the transformative power of God's grace. As pastor, your role is to knit the stories together into a seamless whole, powerfully naming the work of the Holy Spirit in people's lives and stories. It is also an opportunity to authentically share your story of transformation, not as an exemplar, but as a fellow disciple.

Engaging Kids

In today's culture, children are surrounded by messages of condemnation and fear. Bullies actively project messages that make others feel "less than"—like they do not measure up. Use the children's message to counter that narrative. Provide a mirror projecting messages of God's love and grace; affirm each person's worth. As they look in the mirror, standing in front of the congregation, have the congregation repeat this refrain: "[Inset name], You are God's beloved. God loves you and so do we!" Then have the congregation cheer for each child and celebrate their unique contribution to the body of Christ.

Worship Helps

Gathering Prayer

Loving God, rich in mercy, your grace extends to the far reaches of your creation. Your love beckons to us from great distances. As we gather in your name, give us courage to share our stories and give witness to your work in our lives. Help us to hear your voice through one another and respond to your invitation to trust in you. Amen.

Call to Worship (Based on Psalm 107)

From east to west, north to south;
we gather to sing your praise, O Lord.
We come as we are and hear your affirmation,
there is no condemnation. No room for fear.
We thank you, O God, for your steadfast love;
for your wonderful works for humankind.
We come together and bring a sacrifice of praise and thanksgiving.
ALL: And we tell of your deeds with songs of joy!

March 21, 2021–Fifth Sunday in Lent

Jeremiah 31:31-34; Psalm 51:1-12 or Psalm 119:9-16; Hebrews 5:5-10; John 12:20-33

Jennifer and Todd Pick

Preaching Theme

There is an art to letting go, to releasing what is known and safe in exchange for that which breaks us open to new life. Whether we like it or not, we practice this art, with varying degrees of success, all the time. When children learn to walk, they leave behind the world of crawling. When we receive an unwelcome diagnosis, our bodies and schedules surrender familiar ways of being to a "new normal." As pastors, we've been witnesses at bedsides, holding hands when the person in front of us breathes their last and the world stills for a moment in awe and loss. We are all artists who journey with those who have come to the end of one thing and the beginning of another.

By this time in the season, the uncomfortable wildernesses of Lent seem to have outstayed their welcome. We are usually *more than ready* to enter the bright, brassy celebration of Easter, but there are a few things that we must encounter first. We must pay close attention to Jesus's example of letting go because it patterns our communal Christian life together. We are a people who do not proceed from life into death because, as a people of resurrection, we are always walking through death into new life. Over and again, we are asked to relinquish the things that keep us buried in death and to embrace glory and the call to life, afresh and anew.

John 12:20-33 begins with people's universal need to see faithfulness in human form. As Jesus walks a process into Jerusalem over palms strewn under his feet, a few Greeks approach the disciples and say, "Sir, we want to see Jesus" (John 12:21). How many times have you heard your people utter the same sentiment? "We want to see good in the world," "We want to see an end to poverty," or "We want to see each child of God know that they are loved." In a million ways, our people echo the sentiments of the Greeks from two millennia ago. We want to *see* Jesus. But even in our need to see Jesus active and present with us, we need to let go of our notions of just where we think he should show up. This passage, which begins with people needing to see Jesus, ends with Jesus proclaiming, "When I am lifted up . . . I will draw everyone to me" (John 12:32). These men and women who sought Jesus *did* see him with astonished and horrified eyes, lifted up and crucified. Those outstretched arms on the cross and the resurrected life that followed would draw billions into new life through the ages. The difficult truth, though, is that new life only comes from relinquishing the old one.

"I assure you," says Jesus, "that unless a grain of wheat falls into the earth and dies, it can only be a single seed. But if it dies, it bears much fruit" (John 12:24). True to form, when the message gets tough, Jesus moves into concrete application. We often read this passage at funerals, hoping that those who are grieving the loss of a loved one might see the hope of the Resurrection that each small seed brings with it. If the thought of a savior who dies in order to bring new life is too much for us to take in, then a simple seed can help us with the veracity of Jesus's claim. As the seed breaks open, it gives everything of what it was to what it is becoming. And so do we as we practice and perfect the art of letting go.

Secondary Preaching Themes

The scripture from the prophet **Jeremiah** is also about breaking open and letting go. God is in the midst of making a new covenant with the people of Israel and Judah because the old covenant was broken beyond repair. Death to new life: that is our story. That is our song. For the new covenant to take root, God must renounce and forgive the people's past sins and break open their hearts. This open-heart surgery is not meant to harm, but to heal what once was broken with new words engraved on the heart. **Psalm 119** gives close attention to those engraved hearts, keeping God's words contained therein and seeking "with all my heart." Letting go of the brokenness that we carry and allowing ourselves to move from death to new life is at the center of all these readings. How might you embody that movement with all your heart?

Worship Helps

Gathering Prayer

Receive our hearts once again, O Heart of all hearts. Break them open anew with your compassion. Wash them once more with your merciful loving-kindness. In these Lenten days, sow within our hearts the seeds of hope that can turn a valley of shadows into a garden of grace. Lead us onward into the newness of life that can only come from your heart. As we serve and follow you, may grace blossom in our work as we nourish others with words of courage and strength for the journey.

Call to Worship

Seeking the nearness of mercy and grace,
come and lift up your hearts.

We lift them up to the Lord.
Seeking the assurance of love beyond measure,
come and lift up your hearts.
We lift them up to the Lord.
Seeking the fullness of forgiveness,
come and lift up your hearts.
We lift up our hearts, our lives, our all.
Seeking joy and gladness, let us worship the one who makes all things new.

Litany of Response

In our wilderness wanderings,
in the desert places of our lives,
take our hearts, Holy One,
and remake them in your image.
In seasons of struggle and strife,
in words of prayer and promise,
take our hearts, Holy One,
and renew them by your grace.
In our birthing and our breathing,
in our living and our learning to let go,
take our hearts, Holy One,
and fill them with your everlasting life.
In our stillness and our silence,
we make a space for you to enter our hearts…
to create in us clean hearts…
to reclaim, revive, and restore our hearts…

　　　[A moment of silence is kept.]

In our death and resurrection,
in all things, always,
receive our hearts, Holy One,
and hold them in your eternal love.
Amen.

Benediction

Assured of God's promises, written on our hearts,
we go, scattered like seeds, ready to sow love.
Lifted by the Risen One, abiding in our hearts,
we go, scattered like seeds, ready to rehearse resurrection.
Empowered by the Spirit, at work transforming our hearts,
we go, scattered like seeds, ready to rise to new life!

March 25, 2021– Annunciation of the Lord

Isaiah 7:10-14; Psalm 45 or Psalm 40:5-10; Hebrews 10:4-10; Luke 1:26-38

Lydia Muñoz

Preaching Theme

We may find ourselves in the midst of the austerity and solemnness of Lent, only to be interrupted with a little bit of Advent and the story of the announcement of the coming of Jesus to Mary, a young, unassuming girl from Nazareth. I must admit that, as a womanist, this story is rife with trouble and questions for me. Mary's willingness to serve as *theotokos*, or God's vessel, is a beautiful notion of surrender and purpose. However, the other side of this is that the story presents an idealized example of women, which this story (or its interpretation) has placed on women over the years. Mary was the ideal servant who never disobeyed God, unlike the wayward and sinful Eve. St. Irenaeus said that Mary repaired the disobedience of the first woman of creation. She was open, literally, to being "overshadowed" so that through childbirth she could become the holy means of salvation. For all other women, these were big shoes to fill, but we were certainly going to try. Hence, the concept of the *Marianismo Ideal,* which was first introduced by Evelyn Stevens in 1973 and then further expanded by Dr. Rosa Gil and Dr. Carmen Inoa-Vazquez in their book, *The Maria Paradox*, in 1997.

Simply put, it is a traditional concept that a Latina's sole responsibility is nurturing and caring for their family and community. This means that having a career or achieving educational goals is something less than true, or is incompatible with what Mary did. This paradigm means that Latinas are compared to the *Marianismo Ideal* and are made to feel inadequate if one is partially absent from one or more of those roles. Even today, as liberated as I feel I am, and even though I have my partner's full support in reaching any goal I set, the *Marianismo Ideal* has had a lasting effect on me and I often find myself battling guilt after attending long meetings, traveling for conferences, or spending long hours at the church.

Rescuing Mary, and thus other women, from this narrative is probably the best thing you can do as a preacher. Therefore, what if we focus on the surprise of Advent in the midst of Lent, the unexpected, to remind us to expect something from God at all times, and in all seasons? Lent should point us toward something as much as

Advent does. Both can mean that God is birthing something new, even though the process may seem completely different. Mary's willingness to be surprised by God is something to cherish, even for us as we move closer to death. Mary's simple life was about to change forever and, for all intents and purposes, she kind of knew that if she were to choose to be God's vessel, then she would have to deal with the realities of the society around her, much like when we choose to really follow the way of Jesus. Doing so will mean going against the grain and against the norm; it will lead to the end of something in us as we become those who hold the overshadowing power of the Most High.

This is scary stuff, but it can be anticipated joy for what lies ahead. The liberating message for Mary, and for us, continues in this same chapter. We must never see her as a victim or as one who didn't have a choice, but as a poor, young woman who opted to believe that God noticed her, as simple and insignificant as she might have thought herself to be. God does not look away, nor does God forget. God's choice will always surprise us.

Sermon Extras

Doing Justice

Perhaps you might want to follow the thread of uncovering what it means for Mary to be called *theotokos* by most of the Orthodox tradition. Theologian Gregory Palamas argued that Mary was called *theotokos* not because she was perfect but because she was full of grace and full of welcome to the surprising Spirit of God. This made her an open vessel for wonder, power, and the unexpected. One might want to delve deeper into why, as Protestants, we have done such a poor job of honoring Mary's willingness to serve and what a controversial figure she has become over the many centuries among Catholic, Orthodox, and Anglican churches. What can we do to recover some of this work?

Engaging Kids (Based on Isaiah and Connected to Luke)

Do you know what my favorite part of going to the movies is? Well, besides the big tub of popcorn and a box of Milk Duds, my favorite part is watching the previews. They are so cool, and they fill me with anticipation. I get so excited waiting to see what's coming up. (You might want to consider sharing some previews on the screen, if that is available to you. Engage the children and ask them what previews they have seen lately and what are they excited to see that's coming up.)

So today's story is like a preview. We are really far from Christmastime, but today's story is about Advent and Christmas. God is sharing a preview with us.

I think God does this because God knows that waiting is hard. God knows that sometimes, when we are tired of waiting for something to come or for something to happen, it's really nice to hear someone remind us of what we are looking forward to, so that the waiting and the good works we do while we wait don't become too hard.

First, God's preview to Mary helps her see that God wants her to never give up because God was going to do something amazing through her.

Second, God says that what God is going to do is going to be for all people.

Third, even though it's hard to wait, God will never leave her, or us, alone; that's why her son is to be called Emmanuel, God with us.

God's previews are the best!

Worship Helps

Centering Prayer

Let us quiet our hearts and minds as we pray:
come, gentle Spirit.
Refresh and renew us. Stir us and wake us.
Come, calling Spirit.
Lead us and shake us. Call us by name.
Come, powerful Spirit.
Make us courageous and brave. Fill us with determination and commitment.
Come, peaceful Spirit.
Still us and remind us that we are never alone.
ALL: Come, Spirit come!

Psalter with Sung Response (Based on Psalm 40:5-10)

Consider using a Spanish song as a sung response to passages from **Psalm 40**. Information about a recommended song is below. A music leader can sing the song in Spanish first, to introduce it to the congregation. The Spanish lyrics are repeated and easy to learn, even for novice Spanish speakers. To make it even easier, you might alternate between Spanish and English responses.

Recommended Song:
"Cantad al Señor, un Cantico Nuevo / O Sing to the Lord a New Song" is found in *Oramos Cantando: We Pray in Song: A Bilingual Roman Catholic Hymnal.* You can find videos of the song online.

Begin the Psalter with a sung response by singing the entire song.
Leader: You, Lord my God!
>   You've done so many things—
>   your wonderful deeds and your plans for us—
>   no one can compare with you!
>   If I were to proclaim and talk about all of them,
>   they would be too numerous to count!
You don't relish sacrifices or offerings;
>   you don't require entirely burned offerings or compensation offerings—
>   but you have given me ears!

Sung Response—Spanish verse
Leader: So I said, "Here I come!
    I'm inscribed in the written scroll.
    I want to do your will, my God.
    Your instruction is deep within me."
I've told the good news of your righteousness
    in the great assembly.
    I didn't hold anything back—
    as you well know, Lord!
I didn't keep your righteousness only to myself.
    I declared your faithfulness and your salvation.
I didn't hide your loyal love and trustworthiness
    from the great assembly.
Sung Response—English Verse

Make planning easier and more efficient by using these two planning resources!

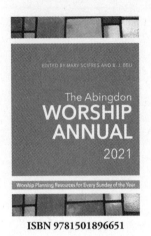

Look for These New Titles from Abingdon Press

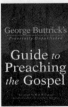

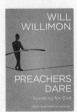

March 28, 2021–Palm and Passion Sunday

Liturgy of the Palms: Psalm 118:1-2, 19-29; Mark 11:1-11
Liturgy of the Passion: Isaiah 50:4-9a; Psalm 31:9-16; Philippians 2:5-11;
Mark 14:1–15:47

Jennifer Quigley

Focusing Prayer

O Lord, my God, give me the tongue of a teacher on this holiest of weeks that I may know how to sustain the weary with a word. Although I may feel overwhelmed with endless liturgies to plan, Easter egg hunts to organize, multiple sermons to write, and all the other labors of ministry looming this week, I ask you to waken me morning by morning— waken my ear to listen as one who is taught. By your Spirit, help me to walk alongside you and bear witness to your journey: from table, to trial, to cross, to grave, and to empty tomb. Amen.

Preaching Theme

I still have vivid memories of being a child on Palm and Passion Sunday, cheer- fully waving my palm at the beginning of the liturgy, relishing in the sight of green fronds waving throughout a packed sanctuary. I also have vivid memories of trying to stand still for the entire reading of the Passion: neck aching from craning over adult shoulders to see something as the reading stretched on, legs itching to move and run around, and feeling overheated from the crowded congregation. In what seemed like a moment, church could turn from delightful to stifling.

Palm and Passion Sunday is a liturgically full moment that contains the heights and depth of the human experience in that it captures the drama and emotion of Holy Week. We begin with Jesus's triumphal entry into Jerusalem. The crowds join in hope and celebration that the future might be better, that there might be a new kingdom, one that is not ruled by the violence of Rome but one in which both heaven and earth rejoice together at God's work in creation. You can feel swept along with the crowd in **Mark 11**, which is the author's point. Together in community, especially in the community of faith, we can hope, imagine, and celebrate in ways that we cannot do alone.

But then the drama turns. The crowds, too, play an outsized role in the Passion narrative. Fears of uncontrollable crowds drawing a violent crackdown from the Roman authorities spur the plot to arrest Jesus in secret. The disciples gang up on the woman with the alabaster jar and they miss the sorrow and anguish of Jesus. And, ultimately, it is the crowds who demand Jesus's crucifixion. You can feel swept along with the crowd in **Mark 14–15**, which is also the author's point. Together in community, sometimes even in the community of faith, we can deny our best selves; give in to suspicion, fear, and jealousy; and we can even enact violence upon one another. Sometimes, spurred by the anonymity of the crowd, we lose our humanity in the most human way possible, by forgetting the humanity of others.

Congregations often have deep commitments to particular liturgical traditions about this Sunday. Some churches do Palm Sunday, barely mark any other moment in Holy Week, and move immediately to the celebration of Easter. It is difficult to stay awake to the suffering of the world around us without an eyes-wide-open look at the Passion. Other churches retell the Passion narrative, often emphasizing the violence of the crucifixion, and miss the more complex human emotions present in this day. It is difficult to find a sustaining word for the weary and some space for hope. Holy Week is both exciting and exhausting for a pastor and it can be asking a lot to try to balance both moments within a single liturgy. But the challenge of this moment in the lectionary, and of this moment at the start of Holy Week, is to create space for the entirety of this drama. If your congregation leans more toward a celebration of Palm Sunday, are there ways to add in elements of the Passion? If your congregation leans more toward a remembrance of the Passion, are there ways to add in moments for literal or figurative palms? Make room in your liturgy for the full range of human emotion and experience that we find in the narratives of Mark 11 and 14–15. And that is the life of faith.

Sermon Extras

Engaging Kids

Many churches invite children to participate in a procession of palms this Sunday. Consider ways to invite children to participate in remembering the narrative of the Passion. Consider breaking the longer reading of **Mark** into sections. Kids can help carry objects that help tell the story of the Passion: a jar of oil for the anointing, bread for the Last Supper, a pillow for when the disciples fall asleep at Gethsemane, coins for Judas's betrayal. Get creative and involve people of all ages in remembering both palms and passion.

Worship Helps

Call to Worship

Precious Jesus, help us to walk alongside you and bear witness to your journey this week: from table, to trial, to cross, to grave, and to empty tomb. Inspire us to work with one another for a world over which heaven and earth rejoice. Give us the strength to never forget your divine image in everyone we meet this week, even when we are swept up by the crowd. Amen.

Benediction (Based on Ephesians 3:18-19)

Throughout this Holiest of Weeks, May [you] have the power to comprehend, with all the saints, how wide and long and high and deep is the love of Christ, and to know this love that surpasses knowledge, so that you may be filled with all the fullness of God.

April 1, 2021–Maundy Thursday

Exodus 12:1-4 (5-10), 11-14; Psalm 116:1-2, 12-19; 1 Corinthians 11:23-26; John 13:1-17, 31b-35

Tanya Linn Bennett

Preaching Theme

Jesus was never afraid to turn the tables, to reverse the roles, or to do the extra-ordinary, outrageous thing. And this passage is a reflection of a final extra-ordinary, outrageous act Jesus performs among the disciples. And perhaps it is because of the outlandishness of this action that we don't count it among our sacramental rituals. Foot washing does not join communion and baptism as our confirmed sacraments. And yet, here in this passage, Jesus clearly ordains it among the most worthy ritual actions: "I...have washed your feet, you too must wash each other's feet" (**John 13:14**). Why have we rejected this ritual to be counted among our sacraments? Is it the humility of kneeling at each other's feet or the abhorrence of touching these appendages, which regularly touch the ground and that might smell or might be less attractive and appealing than other body parts we don't regularly conceal, encased in socks and shoes? Perhaps this is the very reason why we should regularly wash each other's feet.

Peter's response to Jesus's proclamation that he will wash the disciples' feet is equally extraordinary: "No!...You will never wash my feet" (John 13:8). Is it an ex-clamation of horror at the notion that Emmanuel would wash the disciples' feet when certainly the expectation would have been the reverse? Or is it a recognition that this action signals Jesus's understanding that this is their last night together, the night on which Jesus would be arrested and taken away to stand trial and suffer execution by the Roman state? Or is it, perhaps, that Peter is reasoning that, if this ritual does not take place, then the other actions will not unfold either? But, as Jesus responds, if they are not prepared together for both the awfulness and the glory that is to come, then they cannot be joined together in the next place, in the resurrection space.

I am reminded of the **Isaiah 52:7** text, which declares that the feet of the gospel messengers are lovely, gentle, and sacred: "How beautiful upon the mountains are the feet of a messenger who announces peace, who brings good news, who announces sal-vation, who says to Zion, 'Your God reigns'" (NRSV). On this night when we gather to worship, remembering the anguished events to come on this Maundy Thursday, we need to acknowledge that the very word *maundy* means commandment. Jesus commands us here to wash each other's feet, preparing ourselves to join Jesus again in the resurrection life, a life we know is promised and for which we must be anointed properly to enter into. Our feet, metaphorically and physically, are what plant us on holy ground, that bring us to the mountaintop where we can again proclaim the great good news that our God reigns.

Sermon Extras

Engaging Kids

There can be no avoiding a sacramental foot washing. Jesus commands, and we obey. It is one of the most intimate, relational acts in which we can engage in congregational worship life. The traditional means of foot washing involves a one-on-one interaction; one person sits on a chair, submerging their feet into a basin while another person washes and dries. How could it create a different sense of community to have larger pools or tubs set around the congregation in which people could put their feet collectively and then take turns washing and drying? Children could certainly relate to this, as baby pools would be familiar. This type of intergenerational exercise could create a holy sense of bathing together, almost an initiating of our feet into a lifetime of running to the places where the good news is announced.

Worship Helps

Gathering Prayer

Dear Jesus, we offer you our feet, our vehicles to move in this world. Touch them with living waters that we might be the messengers who bring your peace, justice, and joy to a hurting world. Amen.

Invitation to Foot Washing

Loving puts us on our knees.
ALL: We kneel together to serve our neighbors.
Silently washing our feet.
ALL: We kneel together to serve our neighbors.
This is the way we should live with You.

April 2, 2021–Good Friday

Isaiah 52:13–53:12; Psalm 22; Hebrews 10:16-25 or Hebrews 4:14-16, 5:7-9; John 18:1–19:42

Jennifer and Todd Pick

Preaching Theme

Each year we come to this day. It bears a unique burden of grief that confronts the horrific reality of death. We cannot and must not hide, soften, or shy away from its message that sometimes, in some places, it will seem like pure evil has won the day. Every single person in our congregations knows the despair that comes from being in a place like this. The day darkens, and all that is good and right in the world seems to be snuffed out as easily as a birthday candle. If we as preachers don't descend for this one day into the unspeakable pain that comes from injustice, then we are not being entirely true to our calling. This day we look upon the wounds that the world has deliberately inflicted upon those whom it cannot comprehend. We hear the mocking laughter, Peter's trifold denial, the lash, and the crowd yelling, "Crucify, crucify!" and we pause to wonder at how we came to such a moment. Some may want to cover their ears at this noisy story. Some in our pews bear on their own bodies and souls the marks of injustice and crucifixion that still plague our neighborhoods and borders. How could humans made in the image of God be so inhumane?

Into these deep questions of the soul comes the story from the writer of **John**. While there is so much fecundity in the scriptures for this day, make the story the main thing. Let it be your guide as you set about preparing for this day of shadows and darkness. Out of all the gospel writers, the fourth evangelist attributes the most control to Jesus in the lection for Good Friday. There are no desperate pleas from the garden of Gethsemane to "let this cup pass" from him (**Matt 26:39** NRSV). There are no cries from the cross of a savior forsaken. The Johannine Jesus knows his purpose as the living, breathing revelation of God.

Through his dramatic arrest, torture, and crucifixion, the enfleshed Word does not abandon his revelatory nature or his control. As Jesus begins to testify to the chief priest, Jesus makes clear he has nothing to hide: "I've spoken openly to the world...I've said nothing in private" (John 18:20). As the text continues, Jesus has not one, but two, sophistic conversations with Pilate, a reluctant conspirator in Jesus's impending death. He ensures that his mother is cared for and declares with his last breath the completion of his mission: "It is completed" (John 19:30). Everything in order. No broken bones even. Everything done to fulfill scripture. This death was fit for the living Word, who was "in the beginning with God" (**John 1:2** NRSV). This Word—who once endlessly spoke of life and light, ceaselessly testified to truth, and proclaimed a radical union with the divine—falls silent. Our own speech ruptures into silence as darkness and death overwhelm us on this day, and we find ourselves at a loss for words.

However, the story doesn't end on the cross: "Following Jewish burial customs, they took Jesus' body and wrapped it, with the spices, in linen cloths. There was a garden in the place where Jesus was crucified, and in the garden was a new tomb" (John 19:40-41). Take heart that we end this day in a garden. A garden is where seeds go to die, to transform, and to flower. A garden is where the world began. A garden is where the world begins (again). And so shall we.

Secondary Preaching Themes

While it is tempting to cast Jesus into the sole role of the suffering servant from our **Isaiah 52–53** text, ponder how many people are still being crucified in the name of injustice. "Due to an unjust ruling, he was taken away and his fate—who will think about it? He was eliminated from the land of the living, struck dead because of my people's rebellion" (Isa 53:8). How many children of God suffer similar fates today? **Psalm 22** begs for God to come closer. Cries to an empty sky will not stand for this Psalmist who sings of a God who pulled him from his mother's womb (Ps 22:9). If you are utilizing these secondary scriptures, take care to use a theme that testifies to God-with-us in our human suffering.

Worship Helps

Gathering Prayer

Crucified One, on this night of darkness and death, you poured out your love divine to fill our human emptiness. We come to the cross and stand in its shadow. As day falls into night and despair overwhelms us, open wide your arms of grace. As our depravity rooted in sinfulness overwhelms us, open wide your arms of mercy. As words fall into silence and grief and hopelessness overwhelm us, open wide your arms of love. Amen.

Call to Worship

The parade of glad "hosannas" has given way to a mob of violence,
and the path ahead is full of shadows.
Walk with us, O God of light.
Shadows in a garden of betrayal await.
Walk with us, O God of light.
Shadows in a courtyard of denial await.

Walk with us, O God of light.
Shadows of a cross of expediency and death await.
Walk with us, O God of light.
We come to walk the path Jesus walked—from the garden to the court,
from the court to the cross, and from the cross to the tomb.
Help us stand where hope is dying.
Help us keep vigil when the light of love is fading.
Help us walk with you, O God of light.

Words of Hope

The shadow of the cross calls us to face the suffering and brokenness of our world;
to face the sinful injustices that create innocent victims;
to face the forces of evil and the love of power that stand against the power of love.
Lord, have mercy on us.
Christ, have mercy on us.
Lord, have mercy on us.
Truly, truly I tell you:
God suffers with those who are suffering.
God grieves with those who are grieving.
God weeps with those who are weeping.
God labors with those who are laboring for justice.
God sits with us, even in our brokenness.
God is present with us, even in our darkness.
Truly, this is so. And so shall it be. Amen.

Sending Forth

We go forth into a world filled with darkness, but we are not alone.
The One who holds all life and the mystery of death is with us.
We are not alone. We will wait in hope.
We go forth into a world filled with grief, but we are not alone.
The One who holds all hope and the mystery of our faith is with us.
We are not alone. We will wait in hope.
In life, in death, in life beyond death: we are never alone.
The One who holds all love and the mystery of new life is with us.
We are not alone. We will wait in hope.

April 3, 2021–Holy Saturday

Job 14:1-14 or Lamentations 3:1-9, 19-24; Psalm 31:1-4, 15-16; 1 Peter 4:1-8; Matthew 27:57-66 or John 19:38-42

Drew A. Dyson

Preaching Theme

Holy Saturday took on new meaning for me as I sat in the waiting room of a detox center, surrounded by other parents and family members awaiting their first visit with their loved ones who were battling the demons of addiction and facing the precariousness of life. It was Holy Saturday and I still hadn't finished my sermon for the next morning. The strangers in the stark room exchanged knowing glances. The fear and loss loomed thick in the air. Dried tears stained cheeks and breath did not come easily.

The counselor stood in front of the reluctantly gathered group. The cross hung from her neck in shiny protest to the shared dread. "My name is Ana," she said, "and six years, seven months, and eight days ago, I was on the other side of those doors. My parents were here in this room just like you are. And I simply want to say that while you may not feel it today, there is always reason for hope."

I saw Ana as I have imagined Jesus's earliest disciples and followers in the years following the Resurrection. Standing in the middle of life's struggles. Listening compassionately to the pain and fear of friends and families. Sitting with the pain and offering hugs of support and understanding. And offering a simple message of hope: "I was there. It happened. Death did not win."

Holy Saturday is an opportunity to sit with your fellow disciples in the midst of the very real experiences of life. For some, it is a time to name their grief. For others, it may simply be a time to sit in the silence. Authentically share your story of Holy Saturday. Ask powerful questions, such as: "Where do you experience fear in your life?", "Where am I experiencing uncertainty?", or "Where am I grieving or what losses am I living with?" Don't move too quickly toward answers or try to minimize the pain. Simply be. And be together. And, early on the next morning, stand confidently and proclaim the good news: "Christ is risen! He is risen indeed!"

Sermon Extras

Doing Justice

The pain and reality of addiction is devastating individuals and families everywhere. Far too often, the church is silent at best, and a source of condemnation at worst. Use this opportunity to proclaim a different reality. Find a way for your church to get personally involved in supporting people dealing with the disease of addiction. Join your local alliance of civic, religious, and medical professionals trying to fight stigma. Reach out to the local interfaith alliance to initiate a Sunday of healing and hope. Create or host a group for families of addicts. Embody God's love for those locked in the tombs of addiction and sorrow.

Seeking Holiness

Create a sacred place for people to experience Holy Saturday. Open the sanctuary for quiet prayer or prepare prayer stations at the local park. Provide journals and writing prompts designed to draw people into quiet reflection. At varying intervals, gather people together to engage in sacred conversations of listening and support.

Worship Helps

Gathering Prayer

Gracious God, come to us in the silence of this sacred moment and meet us in our fear and doubt. We have laid you in the tomb. We want to cling to hope, but uncertainty holds us in its grasp. We long to hear your voice and your words of assurance and grace. And so we wait. And we listen. But even in the waiting…and the silence…you are there. And that, for today, is enough. Amen.

Sending Forth

The silence lingers. The fear and doubt continue to hang in the air. Still breathless, we rise to leave the sealed tomb. Somehow, through the echoes of uncertainty, we hear a whisper on the wind: "I am with you always. Do not be afraid." And so we arise and go forth in peace. Shaken, but not without hope. For we know that morning awaits and, with it, comes good news. Amen.

April 4, 2021–Easter Sunday

Acts 10:34-43 or Isaiah 25:6-9; Psalm 118:1-2, 14-24; 1 Corinthians 15:1-11 or Acts 10:34-43; John 20:1-18 or Mark 16:1-8

Will Willimon

Preaching Theme

Each of us comes to Easter, the wonder of Jesus's resurrection, from different places in our faith. "Sure, I've believed in the truth of resurrection since I was a child," you may say.

Others of you may listen to my sermon and still say, "I'm just not sure. I don't really believe that I believe."

Some of you may come to this joyful morning full of joy and happiness. Easter Sunday is your favorite Sunday of the church year. You have been rehearsing the music or looking forward with great anticipation to this Sunday for a long time.

Others of you may be in gloom rather than in light. You have just lost someone whom you love. Things are not going well for you at work. And, therefore, there may be part of you that finds all this joy and triumphant gladness to be somewhat oppressive.

And if any of that accurately describes you—believing, not quite believing, full of joy or depressed in grief—then have I got a story for you: the story of the first Easter.

Mary came to the tomb while it was still dark. There is no indication that she brought ointment to anoint Jesus's body, but she knew he wasn't alive. She had been a horrified bystander when Jesus breathed his last (**John 19:25**). When Mary looked in and saw the stone had been rolled away, she didn't shout, "Christ is risen!"

She didn't jump to the assumption of resurrection; no, the whole idea of resurrection was inconceivable to her. Rather, Mary ran to tell Simon Peter and the other disciple, "the one whom Jesus loved," the only disciple who stayed with Jesus throughout the crucifixion (**John 20:2**).

Whatever her explanation, the other disciple looked into the tomb, but didn't enter. Peter, panting a bit, reached the tomb and went inside (John 20:5-7).

Simon Peter saw all these details but comes to no immediate conclusions. However, when the other disciple went in, "he saw and believed" (John 20:8).

When Mary looked into the tomb, she saw two angels who gave her no explanation but rather asked her a rather blunt sounding question: "Why are you weeping?"

Mary replied, "Why am I weeping? They've made off with Jesus's body and I don't know where they have taken it."

Mary turned around and saw Jesus standing there. But she didn't recognize him and assumed that she was seeing a gardener. (Only John located the tomb in a garden.) Mary asked this "gardener" the same question she had asked the angels.

> Mary Magdalene left and announced to the disciples, "I've seen the Lord."
> Then she told them what he said to her. (John 20:18)

So, for Easter we've got a story of three disciples. One sees the grave clothes neatly folded and believes. One sees the same thing but doesn't seem to believe. Another sees but doesn't believe until hearing her name called.

Where are you in this story of the first Easter? I expect that each of us identifies with at least one of these three disciples; maybe some of you identify with all three. Here you are, at the church's celebration of Easter. For some of you, it's quite enough for you to come to church, see the flowers and sing the songs, and you steadfastly, firmly believe, "He is risen!" Others of you come to church, see the flowers, sing the songs, hear the sermon but come away muttering, "I just can't say for sure. I just don't know what to believe." Still others of you see all the evidence, hear the complete testimony and scripture's rationale for believing but you are waiting.

There's a promise implied behind today's Easter gospel: the risen Christ is not here, not entombed in a dead, ancient past. He is risen! He's on the move! Moving toward you, eager for you to see and, in seeing, to believe. He wants to give you what you need in order to believe and is calling your very own name.

I don't care how you came to Easter; Christ's promise is that you won't go away the same. Even amid your questions, doubts, or reservations, Christ will give you the faith to be able to say to the world, in one way or another, "I have seen the Lord!"

Mary comes to the tomb fully expecting to find the entombed, dead body of Jesus. That's not what she finds. Mary persists and is eventually encountered by the risen Christ. Even then, Mary does not recognize him but thinks he is a "gardener." Yet Mary lingers and eventually she sees the risen Christ for who he truly is. The beloved disciple comes to the tomb, then sees and believes. Simon Peter comes, sees, and sort of believes. Three people, all close friends of Jesus, coming and going to the empty tomb in different ways.

We are also told that Mary wept. She stays at the tomb and grieves.

Perhaps it's good to be reminded that many in the congregation come to Easter today, not in joy but in grief. Some may have recently lost a loved one and so they come to Easter in a particularly poignant way. Others may be still dealing with unresolved grief (does grief ever "resolve" in us?) and are hoping to get some insight that will enable them to move forward in life, even in their grief.

While John does not present the resurrection of Jesus primarily as a matter that addresses life after death, the church soon read the resurrection of Christ as a source of hope for our life-after-life. Our hope amid the grief over death is that the same God who raised Jesus Christ from the dead will raise us as well.

Worship Helps

The songs you sing, the music that resounds today, will probably be more helpful in fostering resurrection belief than anything that is said, reasoned, or argued in the sermon.

Gathering Prayer

Jesus, on this grand day you defeated sin and death and rose to new life. In this time of worship, come to us, minister to our fears and doubts and raise us to new life. May we, in this hour, not only sing about your resurrection victory but come to believe in your triumph. May we not only adore you in our worship but follow you forth into the world as we show in our lives and in our words that "We have seen the Lord! He is risen!" Amen.

April 11, 2021–Second Sunday of Easter

Acts 4:32-35; Psalm 133; 1 John 1:1–2:2; John 20:19-31

James F. McIntire

Focusing Prayer

God, resurrect within me a trust in your presence, a discerning spirit, and an openness to your Word within my mind and my heart. Amen.

Preaching Theme

The week after Resurrection Sunday, we are invited into a whole new reality. For Thomas and the others, it starts with the day of Resurrection Sunday. They are locked up in a room somewhere in or near Jerusalem and in some way, Jesus is with them again. Jesus says to them, "Peace be with you," and then he breathes into their lives the ability to forgive, or to hold onto our own and each other's sins (**John 20:19**).

But, Thomas? Well, the "them" in the story is, at first, without Thomas the Twin. He's not in the first scene (John 20:19-23), so he hasn't experienced the power of God's Spirit in this new way and he hasn't come to know the new reality just yet.

The label "Doubter" has been given to Thomas, even though the word *doubt* never appears in the text. Thomas might actually be the only one out of all the followers who was out in the streets already sharing what Jesus had been teaching and doing all along, inviting people into authentic relationships with himself and, more importantly, with each other.

In the second scene (John 20:24-29), Jesus says to Thomas, "No more disbelief. Believe!" (v. 27c) and in the Gospel of John, the concept of *believing* has nothing to do with agreeing to claims and creeds of faith or having no questions or doubts about whether Jesus's body came back to life. *Believing* is the Greek *pisteuo*, which means "to entrust something to another"; it is a synonym for entering fully into an authentic relationship—with Jesus.

Thomas just isn't sure what to believe—what to trust—by the end of John's Gospel. He's not quite sure if he can now be in a relationship with a dead Jesus when he can no longer touch and see the man he's come to know. But of all the followers,

Thomas is the one who didn't run or hide, who stayed around in Jerusalem and did not remain behind locked doors. We don't know which of the other disciples were in the room the Sunday night of the resurrection, or a week later, but we do know that Thomas was because he's named. He stayed around because he wanted to know what was going to happen. Still, the author of John's Gospel blames Thomas for what we call *doubting*.

In *Beyond Belief: The Secret Gospel of Thomas,* Elaine Pagels theorizes that John's Gospel includes this negative story about Thomas because the Christian community that was following the disciple John's teaching was "competing" with the community following the disciple Thomas's teaching. Pagels theorizes that the Johannine community needed a way to discredit the Thomasine community, so Thomas got painted in a bad light in this Gospel. Yet in **John 11**, when Jesus tells the disciples that his friend Lazarus has "fallen asleep" they say, "Let him be" (vv. 11-12, paraphrased). But Thomas insists that they go and experience the depth of the connection between Jesus and Lazarus. In **John 14**, when Jesus lets them know that even when he is no longer around he would not be abandoning them, Thomas is the one who again asks the question, "Lord, we do not know where you are going. How can we know the way?" (v. 5).

Thomas doesn't doubt. He just questions. In all three appearances in John's Gospel, Thomas is The Questioner, not The Doubter, and in the week following Jesus's death, Thomas is filled with questions. Then, on this night, one week later, out come Thomas's questions again. He doesn't doubt that Jesus *could* have been resurrected, he simply doubted the others' story about last week's appearance. He wanted to see it with his own eyes; he wanted his questions answered. Thomas the Pragmatist, Thomas the Realist, Thomas the Questioner—not Thomas the Doubter.

The week before, Jesus had come to the locked room, had stood among them, and had shown them his hands and his side: "When the disciples saw the Lord, they were filled with joy" (John 20:20b). It's no different for Thomas a week later. Not until they saw his hands and his side did they rejoice—not until Thomas gets to see and touch, can he believe.

We all want to touch, see, hear, smell, and taste before we believe or disbelieve. We have questions before we go deep into a relationship with anyone, let alone with Jesus. Thomas was the courageous one who asked rather than simply saying, "I'm full in without any questions."

This believing thing is the point of the Thomas story. It's not what you doubt, but what you believe. As Jesus says: "Do you believe because you see me? Happy are those who don't see and yet believe" (John 20:29); this is the crux of John's Gospel. It's me. And it's you. Can you believe the resurrection stories without having seen the resurrected Jesus? If something happens that is entirely different from anything you might have ever experienced, can you be open enough to allow it to change your life? Can you be in relationship with Jesus without fully understanding the details of the great mystery that is the Resurrection?

Jesus spent his ministry trying to get us to understand that life in its very basic form is quite simply about connecting and loving one another. Period. It is what God desires of us. Anything else makes no difference because when you love one another, justice, mercy, compassion, and peace all follow quite naturally.

Sermon Extras

Dramatic Monologue

This text can lead nicely to a monologue as Thomas shares what has happened in the week following the horrific events of Holy Week. Some questions to consider are: Where has Thomas been? Has he been hiding? What has been said among the disciples? What's next?

Here's the opening of a Thomas monologue, which starts with a generic remembering of a father's hands flowing into Thomas remembering other hands:

For me, it's the hands.

Have you ever looked closely at your own hands? Are they smooth or rough, bent or steady, big and plump or small and delicate?

I remember my father's hands. His job caused lots of tiny little nicks in his hands. And they would dry out quickly. He rarely complained because he worked hard to keep food on our table and clothes on our backs. They would bleed sometimes—a vein close to the skin on the back of his hand nicked by a bump to a rough surface and blood would appear. A bother more than an injury. His fingers were almost smoothed at the tips, as if his fingerprints were fading.

I remember his palms. Deep lines running across the middle like paths tracing the arc of his life's journey.

I remember clearly the feel of his hand when I was little—his large grip swallowing mine as we walked together. I remember the pointing of a finger communicating a stern warning without a word from his mouth. I remember the sometimes rough touch of dried and cracked fingers helping me when my hands needed to be guided or the gentle touch of a hand dusting off a skinned knee and drying a tear.

It's all in the hands.

My friends hands as well—the brothers—John & James, Simon & Andrew. They worked hard too, boats and nets and ropes and fish scales. They rarely complained either. They worked hard; their families ate; they shared all they had with those who had need . . . [1]

Worship Helps

Call to Worship (Based on John 20:19-31)

We question and we wonder, and sometimes we doubt;
Lord, help our unbelief.

We learn and we discern, and sometimes we quickly embrace;
Lord, help our maybe-belief.
We grow and we love, and you call us to be full-in;
Lord, help our growing belief.
"Do not doubt. Only believe," God invite us;
Lord, let us accept.
Lord, be with us from doubt to belief.
Lord, help our belief.
Come, let us worship God.

Sending Forth

Go forth in peace; search, question, act, trust, believe!
My God be always with us! Amen.

April 18, 2021—Third Sunday of Easter

Acts 3:12-19; Psalm 4; 1 John 3:1-7; Luke 24:36b-48

Tanya Linn Bennett

Preaching Theme

My second two children are twins. They were born four weeks early on a stormy, summer, New Jersey night. My daughter was sturdy and strong. My son was also strong, but he was born with a birth anomaly that required immediate surgery. The operation went well, but it caused a respiratory ailment, which made every common cold an uncommonly scary and critical event. The first evidence that a respiratory infection had become serious was that he would stop eating, which was particularly alarming because he had a voracious appetite when he was healthy. So, when he started eating again, we would all breathe a sigh of relief, assured that he was on the road to recovery.

In this passage in **Luke**, Jesus appears again to the disciples. He shows them his hands and feet, proving that he is not a ghost but actually his own flesh and blood. But what really makes him real to the disciples is when he eats the fish that they've cooked. Why is it that Jesus asks for something to eat? Jesus is always proving his identity through the food he shares with those who gather around him. Remember the disciples recognizing him on the road to Emmaus and the breaking of the bread? Remember Jesus cooking breakfast for the disciples on the beach when he reappears? And, as the writer of Luke says, Jesus asks for something to eat while the disciples are "wondering and questioning in the midst of their happiness" (Luke 24:41). Even in the midst of their joy about this miraculous possibility that Jesus has returned to them, the resurrected one, the disciples need more proof. Jesus knows that the disciples need a tangible, recognizable assurance that he is real and truly present with them.

When we eat together, not only at the communion table, but also around tables of fellowship, we remember who we are as a family of faith; we are Easter people. We become more real to each other, more related to each other, more intimate with each other. We prove to each other both our humanity and our divinity.

Sermon Extras

Seeking Holiness

Often after the glory of the Easter celebration, we feel a little letdown. What would sharing a meal of historic biblical food—fish, bread, fruit, olives—do to bring community and fellowship to your post-Easter congregation? Our churches are renowned for potluck dinners, but a focus on foods that Jesus would have eaten might offer an insight into the disciples' experience told in this gospel text in a way that could create insight into that mysterious and magical moment when Jesus reappears to the disciples.

Worship Helps

Gathering Prayer

Let us eat together, recognizing each other in the food we share, in physical food, and in spiritual feeding. Jesus, meet us here. As we share, show yourself to us again. For your faithful and compassionate presence, we are grateful.

Call to Worship (Based on 1 John 3:1-7)

See what kind of love God has given to us?
ALL: That we are called God's children!
Dear friends, now we are God's children, and it hasn't yet appeared what we will be.
ALL: Jesus appears. Jesus shows us what we can be. Let us grow in the love and light of the Risen One!

April 25, 2021–Fourth Sunday of Easter

Acts 4:5-12; Psalm 23; 1 John 3:16-24; John 10:11-18

Kirsten S. Oh

Preaching Theme

When my niece and nephew were about five and seven years old, I had the opportunity to host them for their first sleepover. Among the things they brought to the sleepover, my niece held a pillow close to her chest. They both called it the "mommy pillow." Quizzically, I asked them why they called it that, and I got an image of the extraordinary bond between a mother and her two children. This "mommy pillow" was their actual mom's pillow, which they had confiscated off their parents' bed as they left home. Embedded in this pillow was their mom's scent. They both inhaled the scent and with a broad smile, they both exhaled, "Mmm, mommy smell." In that moment, I realized that they were deeply known, and that they, in turn, deeply knew their mom.

Very recently, I had this same deep sense of being known. My toddler daughter greeted me at the door of our house with a big hug and exclaimed, "Mommy!" Inadvertently, she smelled the coat I had on and said for the first time, "That smells like mommy!"

Whoa—I have a smell too; I have a "mommy smell." I had this exhilarating sense of being claimed—that I am known by this little girl who had already claimed me as her first friend, then her best friend, and now as her mommy with this correlation of smell unique to me. I felt this profound connection with one I've known from the very beginning of her earthly life.

This sense of being deeply and intimately known largely defines one's identity. That is, I am I because I'm in relationship to you who are you. Interpersonal neurobiology shows that unless we see ourselves through someone else's eyes, we can't really know ourselves. That is, healthy human development and functioning happens when the self is relationally integrated with another self.

Martin Buber talks about this relational sense of identity in his salient book, *I and Thou*:

> Love is responsibility of an I for a you: in this consists what cannot consist
> in any feeling—the equality of all lovers, form the smallest to the greatest

and from the blissfully secure whose life is circumscribed by the life of one beloved human being to him that is nailed his life long to the cross of the world, capable of what is immense and bold enough to risk it: to love man [*sic*]. . . . Believe in the simple magic of life, in service in the universe, and it will dawn on you what this waiting, peering, 'stretching of the neck' of the creature means.[2]

I am the good shepherd. I know my own and my own know me.

In this text, the function of the good shepherd laying down his life for his sheep is primarily based on an intimate relationship of knowing and being known. New Testament commentator, George Beasley-Murray, says, "For the Hebrew, knowledge means *experiencing* something."[3] And from this significant knowing, this powerful sense of belonging, Jesus makes this identity proclamation: "I am the good shepherd" (**John 10:14** NRSV).

The contrasts within the parable are the thieves that bring destruction and the hired hands who run off when confronted by wolves. The use of the word *good* to describe his identity as a shepherd has to do with the laying down of his life for the sake of the sheep whom he knows and loves. This is where the word *good* comes in to qualify the role of the shepherd. *Good* in Greek (*kalos*) has multiple translations in this context: "*beautiful, handsome, excellent, eminent, choice, surpassing, precious, useful, suitable, commendable, admirable.*"[4] The act of laying down his life is a beautiful, excellent, commendable, and admirable thing—it is good.

Though the shepherd and sheep may not share the same quality of knowing, nevertheless, it's mutual and reciprocal love in that Jesus lays down his life for the sheep and the sheep recognize and heed the voice of this known shepherd. To know and be known in a relationship reflects the relationship between the Father and Jesus. The good shepherd knows the sheep and lays down his life for them: the sheep know the shepherd and hear his voice and follow in the way of the shepherd.

Sermon Extras

Engaging Kids

Bring a stuffed animal or a toy that you, or someone close to you, loves. Describe the stuffed animal or toy in detail about how it's been well-loved—smell it, touch it, and show the wear and tear of the stuffed animal or toy and talk about how this item is loved. Then ask if the children have or had such a toy.

The shepherd in the story from today's Gospel lesson talks about how Jesus likens himself to a shepherd and how he, as the shepherd, loves his sheep. A shepherd's job is to watch over the sheep, to keep them on the right path, to look for them when they are lost, to love them, to call them by name, to feed them, to bind up their wounds, and to protect them from beasts that can harm them.

Show the children an image of a shepherd holding a lamb with several other sheep surrounding the shepherd and explain that the difference between a shepherd and the good shepherd as portrayed in this image is that God holds each of God's children in God's arms and claims them as God's own. We hear it in this verse from **John**, "I am the good shepherd. I know my own and my own know me" (10:14 NRSV). This shepherd is no ordinary shepherd. He is the most beautiful, excellent, commendable, and admirable one who surpasses even the hard and dangerous job of being a shepherd. The good shepherd knows his sheep one-by-one and lays down his life for them.

Can you imagine yourself as one of these sheep surrounding the shepherd? How would it feel to be surrounding this good shepherd with these other friends in such a bucolic pasture?

Now, can you imagine yourself being picked up by Jesus, being held by him as he whispers, "I know you, I see you, I love you"? How would that feel? What would you say back to him?

Worship Helps

Gathering Prayer

Our good shepherd, you have called us your own.
We come today, celebrating your love for us.
We come today, thanking you for loving us to the point of laying down your life for us.
Shepherding Spirit, move through us, connect us to our identity as ones belonging to you with renewed passion for you and your work.
Amen.

Call to Worship (Based on 1 John 3:16-24)

Beloved, let us not love in word or talk, but in deed and in truth.
By this we know love, that he laid down his life for us, and we ought to lay down our lives for our brothers.

And this is his commandment, that we believe in the name of his son Jesus Christ and love one another, just as he has commanded us.
Whoever keeps his commandments abides in God, and God in him.
ALL: Let us not love in word or talk, but in deed and in truth.

Benediction

May you abide in our Good Shepherd, the most beautiful, excellent, commendable, and admirable one who knows us one-by-one and lays down his life for us, so that we may be an extension of the Good Shepherd by loving one another, just as he has loved us.

May 2, 2021–Fifth Sunday of Easter

Acts 8:26-40; Psalm 22:25-31; 1 John 4:7-21; John 15:1-8

Sudarshana Devadhar

Preaching Theme

At the end of **Acts 8:26,** which reads, "An angel from the Lord spoke to Philip, 'At noon, take the road that leads from Jerusalem to Gaza,'" Luke makes a point, parenthetically, to tell the reader: "This is a desert road." We don't know why Luke specified the time of day, but it might indicate that Philip was called to go out in the heat of midday. In any case, this is a tall order for Philip, which seems to come from out of the blue! The text provides no explanation for the angel's visit. What's more, there is no indication that Philip questioned the angel about either the message or the assignment—Why he should go? Could he do it a little later in the day when the desert heat is more congenial for travel? Was there an alternative route he could take? Wasn't there someone else who could go on this errand or at least accompany him? The text doesn't indicate that Philip raised any objections or asked any questions. It simply says, the angel of the Lord told him to go; "So he did" (v. 27). The lectionary text from Acts for this Sunday offers many sermon possibilities.

One possibility might be to focus on Philip's response to the message of the angel and invite the congregation to consider what it would mean for them, individually or collectively, to respond to such a message, even without knowing where the journey would take them.

Another idea is found as the chapter continues. Philip encounters a man on the road who was different from him ideologically, racially, and culturally. Moreover, he was a high-ranking officer in the Ethiopian government and a eunuch, which made him "ritually unclean" despite his status. When the Spirit told Philip, "Approach this carriage and stay with it" (v. 29), Philip obeyed. Although everything would have seemed strange to him, Philip yielded himself to the Spirit's command.

One of the greatest mistakes of the institutional church is its inclination to let rules and regulations take precedence over the leading of the Spirit. The institutional church's failure to carry out effective evangelism is the result of its tendency to look at the data and figures before it asks the prayerful question, "What is God telling us to do in this particular time and place?"

Another theme can be taken from Philip asking the Ethiopian eunuch, "Do you really understand what you are reading?" (v. 30). The Ethiopian, in turn, asks, "Without someone to guide me, how could I?" and then invites Philip to sit with him (v. 31). A conversation ensues.

Asking a good question often sparks meaningful conversations with others. We live in a "Google age." Social media offers access to religious articles for people of all ages, especially youth and young adults. The questions that are being raised on social media platforms could form the basis for engaging others in a mutual sharing of faith and doubt that deepen relationships. This honest sharing might lead to a new approach to evangelism for the twenty-first century that involves more inquiry, fewer answers, and the building of relationships.

Sermon Extras

Seeking Holiness

A sermon could focus on "Christian Baptism." Once Philip shared the gospel of Jesus Christ with the eunuch, the eunuch was ready for baptism: "The eunuch said, 'Look! Water! What would keep me from being baptized?' He ordered that the carriage halt. Both Philip and the eunuch went down to the water, where Philip baptized him" (**Acts 8:36-38**). What tacit assumptions about baptism does this story challenge? What does it call us to rethink? What does it tell us about the New Testament understanding of baptism? What myths need to be corrected? How do we listen to the Holy Spirit in the midst of theological and ecclesiastical debates about baptism?

Worship Helps

Call to Worship (Based on Psalm 22:25-30)

I offer praise in the great congregation because of you;
I will fulfill my promises in the presence of those who honor God.
**Let all those who are suffering eat and be full! Let all who seek
the Lord praise God! I pray your hearts live forever!**
Every part of the earth will remember and come back to the Lord;
every family among all the nations will worship you.
**The right to rule belongs to God;
The Lord rules all nations.**
Indeed, all the earth's powerful will worship God;
all who are descending to the dust will kneel before their Creator;
my being also lives for God.

Future descendants will serve their Maker;
generations to come will be told about the goodness of God.
They will proclaim God's righteousness to those not yet born,
telling them what God has done.

Benediction

Let us go into the world glorifying our Creator in all we say and do.
May the love of Christ nudge us to go to places we do not want to go,
may the Spirit help us to welcome people we are reluctant to meet,
and may the power of the Holy Spirit move us and shake us
so others may recognize us as people of the living God. Amen.

May 9, 2021–Sixth Sunday of Easter; Mother's Day

Acts 10:44-48; Psalm 98; 1 John 5:1-6; John 15:9-17

Grace S. Pak

Preaching Theme

The scripture passage of **Acts 10:44-48** is the conclusion of Cornelius's and Peter's story of "courageous obedience." Acts 10 opens with Cornelius, an officer of the Italian regiment. The Bible tells us that he was a pious "Gentile God-worshipper" (v. **2**). As he was praying, an angel from God tells him to invite Peter to his house. A short time later, God also ministers to Peter while Peter was praying, by showing him a vision of all kinds of traditionally "unclean" animals and telling him to eat, and then that there will be three men at his doorstep and that Peter is to go with them. Thus, God orchestrates a meeting of highly unlikely people. God calls the church, then and now, to courageous obedience to transform the world through the way Christians love and honor all people whom God created in God's own image.

Cornelius and Peter hear God's message with some trepidation and perplexity but they respond in courageous obedience. So, what does courageous obedience look like?

First, courageous obedience is overcoming the deeply ingrained beliefs and notions that keep us separated from God's people who are different. We grow up learning to fear strangers. We are thoroughly trained to see difference as dangerous and different people as a threat. These deeply ingrained beliefs and notions are called racism, sexism, homophobia, classism, ableism, and so on. Through these, we consciously and unconsciously discriminate against those who are different from us. Those who are different in race, culture, language, class, religion, and gender are socially and systemically devalued and oppressed. Courageous obedience dares us to respond to God's call to overcome all the "-isms" that keep us imprisoned, to tear down the walls of fear that keep us separated, and to embrace and love those who are different, for they are our sisters and brothers in Christ.

Second, courageous obedience is being countercultural. Both Cornelius's and Peter's actions leading to their meeting and sharing Jesus were countercultural in their cultural and religious context. The accepted cultural norms and practices were that Jews and Gentiles, Roman oppressors, and Jewish subjects were in their own corners and did not mingle. Cornelius, a Roman officer, inviting Peter, a Jew who is a subject under Roman occupation, to his house was countercultural. For Peter, a Jew going into a Gentile's house and dining together was also countercultural—it was against religious observance and against the unwritten rule of no mingling. Going against the status quo requires courageous obedience and thus create a holy space.

In their courageous obedience, they created a space for the Holy Spirit to work powerfully, pouring out the gifts of the Holy Spirit to Cornelius and his companions gathered there. More importantly, their courageous obedience provided a learning experience that would change the church for good. According to **Acts 10:34-35**, Peter said, "I really am learning that God doesn't show partiality to one group of people over another. Rather, in every nation, whoever worships him and does what is right is acceptable to him." Courageous obedience changed the mode of ministry of the Jerusalem church and opened the doors to include all people: Jews, Gentiles, and people of all skin colors, cultures, and languages, socioeconomic statuses, and gender identities. Jesus brings the point home: Treat people in the same way that you want them to treat you. In **Luke**, Jesus says: "If you love those who love you [or who are like you], why should you be commended? Even sinners love those who love them or [who are like them]. If you do good to those who do good to you [or who are comfortable to you], why should you be commended? Even sinners do that" (**6:31-33**).

Sermon Extras

Engaging Kids

Briefly tell the story of Peter's vision, showing a few pictures of the animals Peter saw inside the sheet that came down from heaven (e.g., an eagle, alligator, lion, elephant, etc.). God said these animals were good, but Peter kept saying they were not good. This happened three times so that Peter could understand clearly. God wanted Peter to understand that God loves all people and we are to love all people, too.

So how about us? Does God want us to love all people, just as God loves us? Show three to four magazine pictures that represent those in your community who are different, who are not in your church. In what ways is God encouraging you to love people like those in the pictures? How are you being friends to them? What will you do this week to love them? Receive one or two responses. Close with a prayer asking God to give us courage so that we would not be shy but love others and be good friends with them.

Worship Helps

Gathering Prayer

Holy God, your Spirit calls us out of our comfort zones and sends us outside to unfamiliar parts of the community with people who are different from us. And in our courageous obedience, you create space for everyone to experience your presence in powerful ways. Help us to hear your nudging and give us courage to cross boundaries and share the good news of Jesus Christ. May you be glorified in our midst through our acts of courageous obedience! In Christ's name we pray. Amen.

Congregational Prayer

Holy Spirit,
Open our ears so that we may hear you calling us out of our preconceived notions and set ways.
Open our eyes so that we may see all of your sons and daughters regardless of race, ethnicity, culture, and whatever distinction we use to separate ourselves from "others."
Open our lips so that we may proclaim your good news to everyone we encounter.
Open our hearts so that we may love all your people the way you love us.
In Jesus's name. Amen.

Litany (Based on Psalm 98)

Sing to the LORD a new song because God has done wonderful things!
The LORD has made the LORD's salvation widely known.
God has revealed God's righteousness in the eyes of all the nations.
Every corner of the earth has seen our God's salvation.
Shout triumphantly to the LORD all the earth! Be happy!
Rejoice out loud! Sing your praises!
We rejoice out loud altogether with rivers, seas, mountains, and all inhabitants of the earth!
The Holy One will establish justice in the world rightly; the LORD will establish justice among all people fairly.
We shout triumphantly to the LORD and rejoice out loud!
LORD, we sing your praises! Amen.

Sending Forth

In the beginning, God created humanity in God's own image. In the divine image God created them, male and female, light-skinned and dark-skinned, with diverse languages and cultures, God created them. And God doesn't show partiality to one group of people over another. Go out into the world and be an agent of God's love to all people so that your words and actions will be the healing salve for divided and polarized people. May the Holy Spirit empower you to be courageously obedient in your daily walk with the Lord! Amen.

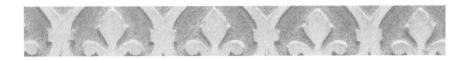

May 13, 2021– Ascension Day

Acts 1:1-11; Psalm 47 or Psalm 93; Ephesians 1:15-23; Luke 24:44-53

Javier A. Viera

[handwritten annotations:]
TRANSmitted hope/good energy for the future / for the day
1) They enjoyed the teachings and enjoyed Christ's ways of — the spoken words
- Inspired & encouraged by his teachings

Preaching Theme

The name and emphasis that we in the church have given to this day is entirely subverted in one simple question asked by the angels in the assigned reading from Acts: "Why do you stand looking up toward heaven?" (**Acts 1:11** NRSV). It's as if they are asking the disciples, and us, how it is that we have so dramatically missed the point of the whole Jesus event. We focus on Jesus's ascension, whereas the angels tell us our focus should be elsewhere.

As preachers we struggle with how to explain these inexplicable events. Perhaps we feel trapped between two equally bad homiletical approaches: either trying to explain how such an event is truly possible or trying to make the story metaphorical and avoid anything that offends the modern, scientific mind. A third, and arguably superior, approach is to focus on the theological claims and significance of this narrative, which is perhaps what the angels were trying to suggest with their subversive question.

The point of this story is not that Jesus took flight. Nor is it enough to say that Jesus simply returned to God to dwell with God in glory. Neither point makes any significant theological claim, and certainly does little to inspire or help our congregants live faithfully or face the challenging moments life inevitably presents. Instead, we might consider making bolder theological claims, such as one made by Richard Rohr, who argues that Jesus didn't go anywhere. He became the universal, omnipresent Christ. What this account from **Luke** makes abundantly clear, especially given the angels' question, is that the point is not to look heavenward, not to make the claim that we too will go to heaven like Jesus to be with God. Rather, what Luke reveals to us is that in Jesus, both heaven and earth are made into one, inseparable reality bound together by the goodness of the God who redeems both. "Why do you stand looking up toward heaven?" is a question that suggests that the real action is right here on earth, and that is where God intends our focus to be. When our focus is heavenward, we more easily dismiss the concerns of the earth and on the earth, and that fails to align with God's intention and purpose in Jesus, who redeems the earth and all who inhabit it. The church should focus its attention and energy here, for this is where God was made fully human, where God offers salvation and redemption, and where God has promised to return and dwell with God's people. We destroy and exploit this planet at our own peril, and we destroy and exploit its people also at our own peril, for God saw fit to give God's self entirely to both.

A second theological claim that merits proclamation on this day comes from Paul's letter to the Ephesians. Paul writes: "I pray that the God of our Lord Jesus Christ, the Father of glory, may give you a spirit of wisdom and revelation as you come to know him, so that, with the eyes of your heart enlightened, you may know what is the hope to which he has called you" (**Eph 1:17-18** NRSV). If in the ascension of Jesus, heaven and earth are made into one, inseparable reality bound together in God (which Paul clearly affirms), then the Christian witness to the world is one full of hope—if by hope we mean living and acting as if God's promises are true. The spirit of wisdom and revelation Paul references in this passage suggests being able to see what God is making known and visible right here on earth. That clearly culminates in God's incarnation in Jesus, but it certainly does not end there. The work continues, in part, because our gaze is not heavenward, but earthly, as together the people of God make real what Jesus taught. Such intentional living has tangible consequences for our life together on earth, and for the planet itself. For in eating together, in building peaceable communities, in being reconciled to one another, in stewarding the resources God has given to us to share as a human family, we become the people God intended us to be. These practices create hopeful futures for people and communities, enable sustainable existence for all and for the planet itself, and manifest the presence of God among us here and now. Jesus's ascension enables us to "know what is the hope to which he has called you" when we too work to make heaven and earth into one, inseparable reality bound together in God (Eph 1:18 NRSV). If we believe that is possible, then it is that hope that we should offer the world and make known in the communities we lead and in which we participate.

Sermon Extras

Doing Justice

Picking up on the theme of the angel's question and giving tangible expression to the idea that in Jesus heaven and earth are made one, this would be a great day to plan a congregation-wide event that exemplifies what this means theologically. While the possibilities are endless, one idea comes to mind: why not use this day to launch a community or church garden project that will benefit families in your community who face the challenge of food insecurity? Caring for the garden and using its produce for the good of others would allow the community to simultaneously steward the earth God has given us and create community with those who are our vulnerable neighbors.

Worship Helps

Gathering Prayer

Loving God, whose Son, our Savior Jesus the Christ, ascended to your presence and glory, grant that we too may ascend in heart and mind to that same presence, that we may be filled with your Spirit and be strengthened to bear witness to your love and mercy on earth as it is in heaven. Amen.

Benediction

May the God of our Lord Jesus Christ, who in him binds heaven and earth together as one, give you strength and courage to be Christ's presence wherever you find yourself this week, so that in you others will know that the peace of God is near and that the kingdom of heaven is at hand. Go in peace to love and serve. Amen.

May 16, 2021–Seventh Sunday of Easter

Acts 1:15-17, 21-26; Psalm 1; 1 John 5:9-13; John 17:6-19

Karyn L. Wiseman

Preaching Theme

One of the most beautiful things about **John**'s Gospel is the imagery and language he utilizes to tell the story of faith. His ability to portray both mundane life experiences and holy teachings is inspiring to many Christians. His Christology is enfleshed in ways that show all persons how God chose to come into the world through Jesus. The biggest difference between the Synoptic Gospels and the Gospel of John is the spirituality that is so prevalent in John. This Christ as "spiritual being" teaches his followers to pray, to live more holy lives, and to be responsive to each other. Augustine is said to have thought the Synoptic Gospels are Gospels "of the flesh," while John's is the Gospel "of the spirit." He was not alone in this description of John's Gospel. It is John who makes mystics, theologians, and spiritualists connect so powerfully to his story of Jesus.

As we read the lesson for today, we are hearing part of a prayerful time when Jesus was preparing the disciples for his imminent departure. This discourse started with the washing of the disciples' feet during their final meal together in **John 13** and it continues to this prayer in chapter 17. This farewell discourse takes up one-fifth of John's entire Gospel. Jesus was concerned for his disciples in this extended prayer, in which Jesus assured them that they were his and that they would always be his. Their calling was intentional, and Jesus was aware of the hardships they would face when he was gone. This assurance of belonging is something many of our listeners are searching for today. Jesus wanted the disciples to be united like he was to the Father (I am typically unwilling to use solely male imagery for God, but the name put in the mouth of Jesus, is indicative of his close familial relationship with God).[1] This prayer spoke to the disciples at the time and would reassure them later on when the story was written and shared with John's community.

We live in a world that is more technologically connected than ever before. We can track a loved one's phone. We can begin (or thankfully end) a group text for family updates. We can locate a restaurant and make a reservation with the tap of an app. These realities should assure us of connection, but they often provide only a false sense of community. Many are looking for a place, a people, a community in which to belong. This is the world we live in. Finding connections through a faith in Jesus can bring about a resolution for that search. In this text, Jesus is reminding his followers that they will not be alone. They have each other and God as they press on to the next events of John's Gospel—betrayal, trial, crucifixion, resurrection, and post-resurrection appearances to Mary Magdalene, the disciples, and Thomas.

Helping your listeners understand the intentional nature of Jesus's creation of community and their own longing for community by creating it, finding it, or being part of it is how we extend Jesus's teachings and create beloved community for all. In the end, Jesus calls on his disciples to bear witness to the truth and to take that truth into the world. And he lets them know, unequivocally, that they cannot separate their love of God and their love of the beloved community.

Sermon Extras

Engaging Kids

We do better in community than we do alone. Bring in a set of building blocks (wooden, Legos, or others) with a flat table or surface to build together. You could even use offering plates to see if the group of kids can build something together. Allowing every child to contribute a block or two to the structure will help ensure that they feel included in this activity. Explaining that we can do more together than we can alone will help connect the kids to an important lesson in the text. We are not alone. This element of doing more together can also lead us to do justice. As communities of faith, we sometimes lose track of the needs around us because we are so focused on our own needs or on our own basic survival. Some congregations serve the wider world by writing checks. Others put their lives and faiths in action to make a difference for others. Finding a concrete way for your community to bond together, collectively, in making an impact in the world is important. Know your context and determine if food insecurity, LGBTQIA+ solidarity, gun violence prevention, or some other social justice issue would spark your people's passion. You can determine what level of engaging ministries of justice fits your context—a postcard campaign to elected officials, marching in a protest, working in a food bank, or creating connections between themselves and those people in need.

Worship Helps

Gathering Prayer

Gather us into this place to receive your word and to be your witnesses to the world during this season of Easter. Bring us to an understanding of true community gathered in the name of Jesus. Help us to live lives that are bound to each other, to all of humanity, and to our created world. Bind us together to share the faith, to care for others, and to be the church in the world. Amen and amen.

Call to Worship

God is present in our lives.
God is present in this place.
We are called to live compassionately.
We are called to live our faith in action.
May we hear the word read and proclaimed.
May we listen to where Jesus leads us to be.
ALL: Amen and amen.

Benediction

As we leave this place, we are called to take the light into the world.
As we leave this place, we are called to love God and one another.
As we leave this place, may we live in unity with God and with one another.
As we leave this place, may we live up to the calling to be community in the world.

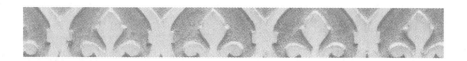

May 23, 2021–Pentecost Sunday

Acts 2:1-21 or Ezekiel 37:1-14; Psalm 104:24-34, 35b; Romans 8:22-27 or Acts 2:1-21; John 15:26-27, 16:4b-15

LaTrelle Miller Easterling

Preaching Theme

"You have demonstrated by your ways and actions that you intend to lead new lives, to the honor and glory of almighty God. Therefore, rise and go in peace, and may the peace of God go with you." I heard these words every first Sunday in my home church, University United Methodist in Indianapolis, Indiana. The Rev. Harry Coleman offered them just after we received Communion. I now recite them as I preside at the table and share the unifying gift of Christ's sacrificial offering. This peace, which Rev. Coleman spoke into our collective consciousness, was born at Pentecost and continues everywhere we allow our identity in Christ Jesus to surpass our racial, cultural, tribal, or even national identities.

The gift of the Holy Spirit poured out at Pentecost is the realization of the promise Christ made to the disciples after his resurrection and prior to his ascension. Throughout what I refer to as "the Appearance Narratives," Christ works to assure the disciples of his identity, the importance of his resurrection, and what will transpire after his ascension. He tells them that they are to remain together until they have received power from on high. As they gathered in the upper room, they experienced God's miraculous movement and heard a linguistic miracle.

This power that comes through the Holy Spirit is the ability to proclaim the great and marvelous works of God in the language of everyone present. In his book, *40 Days with the Holy Spirit*, Jack Levison posits, "The words *God's deeds of power* are shorthand for God's amazing actions throughout Israel's history."[2] Furthermore, the power is magnified because each listener heard the proclamation in his or her own native language. Many of those living in Jerusalem were conversant in Greek or Aramaic. However, within their ethnic groups they also spoke a unique language. It was in those ethnic languages that they heard this proclamation. They were all together, but they heard the miracle distinctly. God created a new identity of unity through the Holy Spirit.

The baptism that takes place at Pentecost is a baptism into selflessness and humility. It is a selflessness born of witnessing God pour blessings upon all those gathered without exception. This baptism reorients our thinking and reanimates our very being. While we acknowledge our diversity as unique representations of the *imago Dei*, those differences do not necessitate division. Division is caused by a belief in scarcity of resources or in the belief of superiority of one group over another. The Holy Spirit demonstrated that all are equal and that there is enough for all. Those who understood God's faithfulness in Israel's history also knew they could trust God to be faithful in the future. They were transformed. As articulated by Father Richard Rohr, "A transformed person is a participatory self, an inclusive self, a generous self, revealing a measurable move toward compassion—and beyond protecting one's personal autonomy and small, egoic reference point."[3] As a people of Pentecost, do we model this kind of unity? What does our tendency to still worship or gather in homogeneous groups witness about our faith? Are we willing to hold all of God's creation in common?

In our present climates, both secular and sacred, the tendency is to draw lines. The lines correspond to our predetermined ideas of who is worthy and who is unworthy; who is holy and who is unholy; who is true to the word of God and defiles the word of God. Within denominations we see lines being drawn through talks of schism and the tension between preserving tradition or being open to an evolving theological understanding. As the celebration of the Festival of Weeks was underway, a Jewish tradition to give thanks for God's provision of grain, a new manifestation of God occurred. During the marking of God's former activity, God birthed a new outpouring of God's provision by setting the Holy Spirit loose upon those who were expectantly gathered and waiting. This Holy Spirit arrived with tangible evidence that something different was occurring. Neither the wind was new nor the fire, but the phenomenon of diverse languages being spoken by a peculiar people was quite new. It was so new that, at first, it was mistaken for drunkenness. Those who spoke were Galileans, a people not highly respected or regarded. These are the people with whom God manifested Joel's prophecy. Would we accept a revelation of God from the marginalized today?

Sermon Extras

Seeking Holiness

The theme of birthing a new creation is continued in the Romans lectionary passage. Believers await the full manifestation of God's promised salvation in Christ's second coming. As they wait, they struggle with the content of their prayers. Authentically achieving unity is easier said than done. How do we pray beyond our own self-interest, beyond the needs of our community? How do we pray for a blessing that transcends personal, cultural, and even geographic boundaries? How do we move beyond a theology of scarcity and favoritism to one of expansive and extravagant grace and blessing for all?

Invite the congregation to enter into a covenantal partnership with another congregation from a completely different culture or religion. This covenantal relationship could include times of study, mutual sharing and listening, and mission projects. It could also mature into joint advocacy and action. Invite participants to share how they are experiencing the word and the world differently as they grow in fellowship and affection for one another.

Worship Helps

Gathering Prayer

Holy and transforming God, set us on fire. As we celebrate the birth of the church on this Pentecost Sunday, may our desire to boldly claim our identify as Christ-followers be like fire shut up in our bones.

A Prayer at Pentecost

Holy God,

How long until we believe your word, O God?
> You do not privilege male over female, nor female over male.
> There is no master race, no peoples more beloved than another.
> No being was created to be enslaved, nor to live in forced servitude,
> nor to be perpetually imprisoned in abject poverty or unrelenting squalor.
> Your blessing fell and falls on all without reservation.

How long until we live your word, O God?
> Courts, councils, and countries cannot bestow on humanity
> more dignity, worth, or status than your image imparted to all flesh.
> There exists no creed, constitution, or covenant that supersedes
> your divine will for equality, equity, and egalitarianism.
> May our practices fulfill your prophecy on earth as it is in heaven.

How long until we teach your word, O God?
> May we cease devaluing, demeaning, and destroying one another
> through our action, inaction, and indifference.
> From the pew to the pulpit to the parking lot may our words resound
> with your truth that all flesh—all flesh—is beloved and beautiful in your sight.

This is our prayer at Pentecost.
This is our prayer for Pentecost.
This is our prayer after Pentecost.

Amen and amen.

May 30, 2021–Trinity Sunday

Isaiah 6:1-8; Psalm 29; Romans 8:12-17; John 3:1-17

Heather Murray Elkins

Preaching Theme

Post-Pentecost Sunday. The Christian year moves from Acts' fiery narratives of power and light, to the celebration of a complex doctrine: the Trinity. The **Isaiah** text, with its scorching heat and prophetic call, or **John's** night vision of Nicodemus's new birth extend preaching possibilities on the Spirit. The trinitarian connections would need to be constructed, but the **Romans** passage offers an invitation to immerse ourselves again in the baptismal life that is water-marked by the triune God.

Here, Paul is teaching the community how to live the mysteries of the sacramental life into which they have been received. This text is orthopraxy for those who have been baptized in a discipleship of freedom, a community of equals. Jew and Greek, slave and free, male and female (**Gal 3:27-28**) are labels that come off in baptismal water. We are now brothers, sisters, siblings in Christ. In this rite of initiation, our identity is confirmed by the naming of God's identity. In whose name are you baptized? This naming of our triune God is essential for our identity as Christians. It is not a "formula," but a formative naming of all those who bear *imago Christi*, the image of Christ. It is a scriptural, theological, and emancipatory proclaiming of identity.

Distinctions based on privileged power dissolve as we are immersed in the life of the One who is Three. Yet the uniquely created *imago Dei* in each human life is not washed away. This is not a spit-and-polish action; this is a dying-and-rising approach to human transformation. This is a rewriting of the genetic code: strangers and neighbors, aliens and alienated are now brothers, sisters, siblings. We are family. We are one in the Spirit.

Yet our baptismal oneness is modeled on "the irreducible diversity of the triune God" whose image we bear, as Marjorie Hewitt Suchocki writes in *God, Christ, Church: A Practical Guide to Process Theology*.[4] This holy human image must be discernible in the daily actions of those who claim baptism. We do not "belong" to ourselves any longer. We are now part of the irreducible diversity in the commonwealth of a God who is also in community. This is relationship writ large. The *shalom*, the life, health, and peace of each is the responsibility of all.

As we read in Romans: "So then, brothers and sisters, we have an obligation, but it isn't an obligation to ourselves to live our lives on the basis of selfishness" (8:12).

Obligation is not an easy word on which to preach because it's a tough word to live with. It's a moral or a legal requirement. It's a duty assigned, or an order given. It's definitely a relationship, and in its third definition, we find Paul's freedom and grace. An obligation is a debt of gratitude. It's a willingly accepted indebtedness. We love because we were first loved. We practice hospitality because we were once nobody and now we're somebody. We're set free for service because God so loved the world.

Trinity relationships are ties that bind and loosen at the same time. We are family because we've been adopted by the triune One whose nature and name is Love. We're no longer shuffled from one temporary shelter to another. We can never be forcibly separated or caged away from the nurturing love of Abba as known to us in Christ Jesus through the Spirit. We're wanted, chosen, welcomed. Our service is not slavery; we are not forced to work for less than a minimum wage of respect. Our life is funded by extravagant love of the triune God who creates, redeems, and sustains us. We are heirs, not by right, not by ancestry, but by grace.

Baptism into the triune life of God marks every man, woman, and child like a permanent tattoo: *imago Christi*. But this mark can only be deciphered when a baptized community demonstrates the life, liberty, and love of the One who is irreducibly diverse. We are not free of obligation; we are free to live our lives without fear. We do not fear diversity as a threat to community because the nature of God, Abba, Christ, and the Holy Spirit is "irreducible diversity in community."[5] We have a spirit that shows we are not alone because we know we're not our own.

Sermon Extras

Engaging Kids

Consider teaching children (and adults) in your congregation the Trinity Creed:

Tradition comes from the word *traditio* and it means to hand on the creed. This is, and was, the teaching responsibility of the community for all young believers. This children's word is a hands-on exercise in doctrine, a teaching of the creed, that will enable children (and the child in every adult) to experience and communicate the essential relationship that is called the Trinity. It requires one adult to teach the children and a congregation willing to participate in the exercise so that they can reinforce the lesson with the children throughout the year. The leader should be facing the children and ask them to hold up both hands showing their thumbs, index fingers, and middle fingers. As the words are recited by the leader, the fingers are lifted and lowered. Encourage the children to repeat after the first time through. The second time through, the congregation should be invited to join in.

Three (thumb and two fingers up) is One (thumb and middle finger down), and One is Three (all fingers back up), and the One in the middle (index finger alone) created me (point index finger toward chest).

Three is One and One is Three
and the One in the middle
died for me (make sign of the cross with index finger).

Three is One and One is Three,
and the One in the middle
sets us free (raise both hands above head).

The second verse of the chant can be alternated to match the Christian Year, as follows. Christmas: "The One in the middle was born (rocking motion) for me"; Easter: "The One in the middle was raised (finger lifted upward) for me"; Advent and Christ's Return: "The One in the middle will come for me" (arms crossed with index fingers pointing toward shoulders).[6]

Worship Helps

Gathering Prayer

You are beyond our grasp,
yet closer than our breath,
refresh your Holy Spirit in all who gather
to share in the gifts and the obligations of love.
You have chosen us;
give us the courage to claim our new name, "Beloved."
Bind us to Jesus and free us in service with and for all.
Amen.

An Offering

Most giving God,
accept this offering from our lives.
In God we trust.
Lord, we believe. Help our unbelief.
Dedicate these gifts to holy human use.
Take what seems ordinary:
a handful of coins, some cash, a collection of checks,
and make them be for others evidence of love that's seen.
Accept what we hold up for blessing,
for we offer ourselves in union with Christ's offering for us.
Amen.

Sending Forth

Abba, your Beloved taught us to pray.
Help us to live as family, forgiven and free as we follow the way.
This we ask in the name of the Father, Son, and Holy Spirit,
one God, Mother of us all.[7]
Amen.

May 31, 2021–Visitation of Mary to Elizabeth

1 Samuel 2:1-10; Psalm 113; Romans 12:9-16b; Luke 1:39-57

Meredith E. Hoxie Schol

Preaching Theme

Recently, I was introduced to the concept of *en cojunto* by an organization whose mission it is to mentor and support Latinx scholars studying theology and religion.[8] Translated into English, *en cojunto* can mean "as a whole," "jointly," or even "bodily." But as is often the case, these direct translations do not adequately capture the ways this concept is employed to frame the deep communal commitment to those in our communities of care. There is something far more profound behind this concept than a simple definition. The power of living *en cojunto* is central to the flourishing of Latinx communities, as it infuses individual experiences of struggle with collective histories of resistance and resilience.

In my most recent reading of Mary's visit to her cousin Elizabeth, I was struck by the ways this shared experience—not only their mutual experience of unexpected pregnancy but also the experience of being physically together to name their experiences—helps to widen their understanding of the significance of this moment. Rather than focusing on the ways their individual lives are certain to be turned upside down by these children they are carrying, collectively they call each other to remember God's upending action in the history of their people and in the world. They remind each other of the promises of a God who has brought and continues to bring new and radical ways of being into the world.

The laboring that Hannah and Mary conjure in their prayers—the anticipated birth of a new baby and the ongoing struggle to bring about the upended kingdom of God—speaks to both a laboring for new life and a new world order. Both are exhausting. Both require bodily struggle, and we count ourselves blessed to take on this work "jointly," with those in our communities of care as we strive to live and thrive. It is work we do *en cojunto*.

Mary's song reverberates with the hopes and dreams of our earthly anticipation. The fact that she sings it in Elizabeth's presence reminds us that we never labor alone. She reminds us to turn to our communities of care and carry on this work *en cojunto*, alongside those who call us to remember our collective struggle, both for life and for liberation.

Sermon Extras

Engaging Kids

Invite the children to think about a time when things didn't go the way they planned. You can offer examples such as:

Maybe you thought you were going to go to the park after school but your parents had to change plans.

Maybe you studied for a test, but then you were surprised by some of the test questions and you didn't do as well as you thought you would have.

Framing the question: To whom did you turn to talk about how you were feeling? (Did you talk with your friends, parents, or teachers?)

Talk together: In addition to the fact that we have family, friends, and teachers who help us when things don't go quite the way we planned, we also serve a God who has helped guide people and tribes through challenges for generations. Mary and Elizabeth were both surprised when they found out they were going to have babies, but they also reminded each other that God was with them, even when things caught them off guard.

Next time you feel like something isn't going your way, I hope you will continue to turn to _____ (friends, parents, and teachers). And maybe you can ask them to tell you a story from the Bible (maybe it is this one about Mary and Elizabeth) about a time when God helped people out, even when things didn't go the way they expected.

Worship Helps

Gathering Prayer

God of life,
We come to you today still basking in the light of the fire of Pentecost. As we continue our praise and celebration of the birth of a new church, we pray today with Hannah, Elizabeth, and Mary who knew well the excitement of bringing new life into the world. These women remind us of the joy and responsibility of laboring for a new life and a new world —a world all mothers hope for, where those who are hungry are full of good things and those who abuse their power will be brought low.

May we find inspiration in their courageous prayers, and may their words help us to find encouragement and strength for the hard work of laboring for a more just world. Amen.

Call to Worship (Based on Psalm 113)

Blessed be the name of the LORD,
from this time on and forevermore.
Today and forevermore, we bless the name of the Lord together.

From the rising of the sun to its setting
the name of the LORD is to be praised.
Today and every day, we praise the name of the Lord together.

The LORD is high above all nations,
and his glory above the heavens.
In this place and in all places, we give glory to the Lord together.

Praise the Lord.
Let us praise the name of the Lord together.

Benediction

Receive this benediction from Mary's song:
The LORD makes the poor and makes the rich;
    he brings people low, he also exalts.
He raises up the poor from the dust;
    he lifts the needy from the ash heap,
to make them sit with princes
    and inherit a seat of honor.
For the pillars of the earth are the LORD's,
    and on them he has set the world.

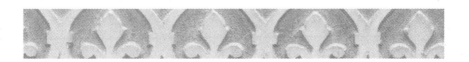

June 6, 2021–Second Sunday after Pentecost

1 Samuel 8:4-11 (12-15), 16-20 (11:14-15) or Genesis 3:8-15; Psalm 138 or Psalm 130; 2 Corinthians 4:13–5:1; Mark 3:20-35

Kathleen Stone

Preaching Theme

I've heard the phrase "All of life is a gamble," yet we act as if the well-intentioned gambling we do is assured and under our control.

We do this and this should be the return; we purchase something we think is a good deal and then it falls apart. We buy something for our convenience, but it's actually made from things that are horrid for us and for the environment, which makes life much harder for someone else, and even for ourselves. If we have a little money, then we put money in the stock market or in the bank and then it fails to grow. We decide on a healthcare plan and it's not what we expected. Over and over again we take risks. Every day. As we walk out the door, anything could happen outside those walls, or with the next person we encounter. Anything can happen. We become used to taking it all into our own hands, relying on our own strategies and wits. Some of us think we live in a society that obligates itself to be fair, and if you just do it right, then it will be right. Yet, this is not the truth. Some of us know that this is not the case and figure out other ways to make ourselves more secure, at least a little bit. By our own wits and time after time, throughout our lives we think and strategize that if we do "this," then we will have "this much." We live in a society that has told us it's up to us and we'll be alone to succeed or fail in our efforts. Yet, it simply is not true.

What risks were the people in these scriptures about to move into and how different is all that strategic thinking to what we do every day? And what is it about that kind of negotiation, that kind of taking it into our own hands, that keeps us from relying on God for our very lives?

After reading about how the elders of Israel in Samuel strategized to have a king rather than a prophet as their governance, or reading about how Adam and Eve risked disobedience thinking they'd get ahead, we realize that both of these stories share how God's way is *the way*, and if we just back up into God's arms, then we will find our true security. In today's Gospel, Jesus took a risk. And it was a risk that, we see now, reveals to us a lesson about God's ways. We see Jesus actually making a decision that was not about his own success and ensuring that everything goes well. Rather, Jesus's decision came about because deep in the well of his gut, he knew that his mother and brothers were unaware of the God he was talking about and that more than providing security based on pleasing them, he needed people who understood that. And so Jesus, without hesitation, looked up and said, "I know who I am and I know what works. And what works, is collaborating with God for God's kingdom on earth, not Saul's kingdom or my mother's kingdom. Then, all will be well with our souls."

However, we keep taking risks to get a better deal, don't we? We strategize because we think we know what we need and what will feed us better. That's the action of the people in **Samuel**. That's the action of Adam and Eve. That's the action of Jesus. It's not doing nothing; rather, it is aligning ourselves with the security we find in knowing we are children who are subject only to the love of our Creator. So often, we trade the author of our salvation for a much lesser god.

A Reading of **Psalm 138** would be very appropriate—either in response form or with a dramatic voice of someone who memorizes and shares the psalm with the congregation.

Sermon Extras

Engaging Kids

Read from the **2 Corinthians** passage: "For we know that if the earthly tent we live in is destroyed, we have a building from God…not built by human hands" (5:1 NIV). Then read the story "The Three Little Wolves and the Big Bad Pig" by Eugene Trivizas and Helen Oxenbury.

Ask children this question: What did the little wolves finally do differently? Why did that save them? What does a building from God look like?

Doing Justice

Go visit a detention center, a soup kitchen, or a food pantry and ask those who are facing the bottom rung of the system we currently live within this question: How do they see God in their lives, and how has it changed over the years?

Nurturing Creation

How can we know that God and God's creation, and its original laws, are critical for our collaboration? How much of the wreckage of creation has been brought about because we have actually sought to build our own security rather than rely on God?

Worship Helps

Call to Worship

Lord, open our lips
and our mouths shall praise you.
Lord, open our ears
and our ears will hear your voice.
Lord, open our hands
and our hearts will serve You.

Congregational Prayer

God of love, teach us how to rely on you. As we continue to strategize in our lives to get ahead, to provide for our own security, to make sure it all goes well for us and our families, help us just to stop, breathe, and remember the holy story of your death and resurrection. Help us to remember that you come not as we expect but in the craziest ways. Help us to remember that we need only to focus on loving you, ourselves, and others. Give us grace when we fail and help us to know that it is only in you that we really find the abundance we seek. In Christ's name we pray. Amen.

Offering Prayer

What does it mean to come before you, Lord Christ? What do our lives consist of without you, our church, or the fellowship of those who desire a deeper connection to you—where their hands and feet stretch out to the ends of the earth? Take these pennies and make them work for you, here, there, and in the outer reaches, for you are surely our first love and our redeemer.

Closing Prayer

God of grace, you are the secure place in our lives. Be with us as we so often thrash our arms and restlessly flail our legs in this search. Help us into the calm of your heart as we continue this journey into your kingdom. Help us to be the people who know that, even when all of life swirls around us, you are present. Thanks be to God.

June 13, 2021–Third Sunday after Pentecost

1 Samuel 15:34–16:13 or Ezekiel 17:22-24; Psalm 20 or Psalm 92:1-4, 12-15; 2 Corinthians 5:6-10 (11-13), 14-17; Mark 4:26-34

Ernest S. Lyght

Preaching Theme

The idea of doing the right thing is a recurrent theme in the epistle text of **2 Corinthians 5:6-10 (11-13), 14-17.** Paul desires that his hearers engage in living a life that pleases God. As a disciple of Jesus Christ, one is on a journey that leads home, and our home is with the Lord. The pilgrim journey is a journey that is based on trust in God: "We live by faith and not by sight" (2 Cor 5:7). There are things in life that we cannot see, such as wind, electricity, and air; however, we depend on them all. Paul calls on us to have confidence in what is but is not seen. Such seemingly invisible forces are dynamics like trust, grace, faith, hope, and love. Our confidence should not shrink in any circumstance, whether one is "at home" or "away" from either "the body" or "the Lord." The right thing on the Christian journey is pleasing God. On the journey, one encounters good and bad things; however, it is God who solves the equation, the positive and the negative. In the earthly life, Paul calls for doing the right thing, to be mindful of the reality that one day "we all must appear before Christ in court" (2 Cor 5:10).

This passage reminds us that we are the recipients of the invisible power of God's love. In this modern age, we tend to rely on our GPS while driving. In life, it is more beneficial to rely on God's positive steps. In a conversation with Jesus, Thomas noted that they did not know how to get to the place where Jesus was going. Jesus said: "I am the way, the truth, and the life" (**John 14:6**). It is helpful to keep our focus on Jesus as we travel. On one occasion, Peter in the midst of a storm dared to approach Jesus by walking on the water. Jesus invited him to come forward, knowing that Peter would be OK as long as he kept his focus on Jesus. The moment Peter changed his focus, he began to sink into the stormy sea (**Matt 14:28-30**). Paul invites us to keep our focus on Jesus and to avoid dangerous water. It does not matter what other people think of you. Paul was very comfortable with being himself: "If we are crazy, it's for God's sake. If we are rational, it's for your sake" (2 Cor 5:13). Today as then, we have a vital ministry of reconciliation.

Paul touts the idea that "the love of Christ controls us" (2 Cor 5:14a). Furthermore, God's love is at the center of our ministry. Christ died for all of us. So, we live for Christ (see 2 Cor 5:14-15). The most important thing is what is in one's heart (2 Cor 5:12b). Paul had tremendous passion for Jesus, whom he did not meet in the flesh, but Paul had persecuted many of Jesus's followers. His knowledge about Christ's death and resurrection keyed a change in his understanding and theology: "So then, from this point on we won't recognize people by human standards" (2 Cor 5:16a). Paul points out a change in viewpoint, acknowledging that, although they once knew Christ by human standards, now they no longer use such human standards. Paul was changed when he encountered Christ on the road to Damascus (**Acts 9:1-22**). First, Paul's human point of view justified his persecution of Christians by imprisonment and even death. God opened Paul's eyes and gave him a new lens from which to view Christ's followers. Paul learned how wrong and cruel human judgment can be. Second, Paul's warped view of Christ was miraculously changed in a dramatic way. Paul's new vision enabled him to focus not only on the crucified Jesus but also on the risen Christ. It could be said Christ's love transformed Paul's view of all people. Listen: "So then, if anyone is in Christ, that person is part of the new creation. The old things have gone away, and look, new things have arrived!" (2 Cor 5:17). The language of new creation is anchored in Isaiah's words (**Isaiah 65:17; 66:22**). Surely, this was Paul's personal Pentecost. In Christ we are a new creation, reconciled to God. We are agents of God's reconciling love for all creation. How, then, do we do the right thing and stay grounded in God's love?

Sermon Extras

Engaging Kids

"Doing the right thing" is the theme that weaves its way through these Pentecost lectionary texts. In **1 Samuel 15:34–16:13**, we observe that Samuel followed the Lord's instructions and went to Bethlehem. In selecting and anointing David as the new king, Samuel learned that God does not look at things as humans see them. In 1 Samuel, we read: "Humans see only what is visible to the eyes, but the LORD sees into the heart" (16:7c). This notion is reflected in the **2 Corinthians** text (5:16). The **Ezekiel** text further reminds us that God is in charge, choosing to take a cedar sprig and plant it. It is God who lifts up Israel. The same idea is expressed in the **Mark** text, painting a picture of God's kingdom, which is like both the scattered seed that matures and the small mustard seed that grows into a large tree. These texts demonstrate possibility in God's activity, growth, and fruit.

A children's sermon could capture the essence of "doing the right thing" by focusing on the idea of choice. Questions to ask are: How do you choose the right activity, friend, or behavior? What does the Bible teach us about making good choices?

Worship Helps

Call to Confession (Based on Psalm 20)

The psalmist reminds us that it is a good thing to go to God in confession: "Let God send help to you from the sanctuary and support you" (Ps 20:2). God knows about your sacrifices and offerings. God knows what is in your heart. Allow God to "fulfill all your plans" (Ps 20:4). So ask God by expressing your requests, and trust God.

Benediction

Sisters and brothers, as God's kingdom workers, go out and sow God's word in every place available to you. God will nurture the seeds. Get ready for the harvest and gather the fruit.

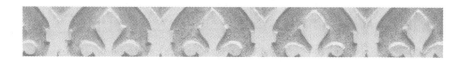

June 20, 2021–Fourth Sunday after Pentecost

1 Samuel 17:(1a, 4-11, 19-23) 32-49 or 1 Samuel 17:57–18:5, 10-16 or Job 38:1-11; Psalm 9:9-20 or Psalm 133 or Psalm 107:1-3, 23-32; 2 Corinthians 6:1-13; Mark 4:35-41

Sheila M. Beckford

Preaching Theme

Giants! We all have them. When going through hard times or crises in our lives, it seems as if the obstacles are giants. We try to avoid them. We make up excuses. It is fear that prevents us from forging forward and addressing the issues at hand.

Today, the story of David and Goliath helps us challenge those giants in our lives. David, probably a young, scrawny boy with no skills for fighting a warrior, enters the scene. Not only does he see Goliath but also he hears his challenge to the Israelite soldiers to a one-on-one, winner-take-all battle. Goliath was a giant compared to the others. He was nine feet tall (depending on the biblical translation), a champion, and undeniably strong. He went to war in armor, including his helmet and spear, which weighed over 140 pounds. To the Israelites, he was unstoppable. He too believed he was unstoppable. He was much bigger, stronger, and bolder than all of the Israelite soldiers. The Israelite soldiers, including Saul (their leader), were afraid to take on the challenge. To lose would not only give the Philistines bragging rights but also the Israelites would lose their property, livelihood, and freedom.

As the story continues, David steps up. He refuses to wear Saul's armor because it was not what he was used to. Instead, David put on the armor of God, and with God by his side, David slays Goliath! For some, this is the story of the underdog entering the battle with uncertainty and coming out victorious. Many seem to love the underdog story, but this is more than just about David-the-underdog winning! For me, this is a story about self-reliance versus God-reliance.

When Saul challenged David's ability to combat this professional warrior, David's response was, "The LORD . . . who rescued me from the power of both lions and bears, will rescue me from the power of this Philistine" (**1 Samuel 17:37**). It was with God's help that David was able to slay his giant. While Goliath relied on his own strength, reputation, and warrior skills, David relied on God's power, reputation, and using

–95

David's defensive abilities. The giants in our lives may be too big for us to defeat by ourselves, but when we rely on God to use the skills we already possess, our giants will fall.

Our giants may not be a man standing nine feet tall and adorned in brass armor, carrying a spear, but the threat is the same. Our giants are powers and principalities. Our giants block our light and prevent us from seeing our way. Giants take our breath away so that we can't breathe. They cause us to find ways to hide from them instead of eliminating the threat. The story of David and Goliath reminds us that if we rely on God, then we will not need to hide in the darkness or lose our breath, but rather, all will be redeemed. In the battle between self-reliance and God-reliance, God will win every time. That same power will rescue us from the giants in our lives, whom we are afraid to confront and address.

Sermon Extras

Seeking Holiness

We all have giants in our lives. Our current political climate is a giant, poverty is a giant, racism is a giant, climate change is a giant, the justice system is a giant, and immigration policies are giants. However, these are only some of our giants. Many organizations were developed just to tackle these giants. We cannot do this work alone. Like David, God uses the skills that we possess to defeat the giants that continually oppress God's people. Goliath represented oppression, while David represented God's light of freedom. What God-given skills were you given to assist your community in fighting against these giants? Let God use your unique skills and attributes to challenge the status quo and thus transform the world.

Worship Helps

Call to Worship

Holy One, we are strong
because you are strong.
We are fearless
because you are fearless.
We are holy
because you are holy.
ALL: We are strong and of good courage. We give thanks to you, Lord, for your wonderful deed for humanity. We are redeemed! Amen!

Sending Forth

Christ, our redeemer, we thank you for delivering us from the storms of life. Help us now to go out into the world, sharing our faith with our community. Now, with the power of the living God, go into the world, shining God's light into the darkness. Go, transform the world!

June 27, 2021–Fifth Sunday after Pentecost

2 Samuel 1:1, 17-27 or Wisdom of Solomon 1:13-15, 2:23-24 or Lamentations 3:22-33; Psalm 130 or Psalm 30; 2 Corinthians 8:7-15; Mark 5:21-43

Karyn L. Wiseman

Preaching Theme

The Gospel of **Mark** has always slightly frustrated me. The "Messianic Secret" the author uses can create the misconception that those who followed and heard Jesus were just too clueless to fully understand his purpose. Jesus's true identity was kept secret as a device until the author could portray that all were ready to understand Jesus's message and ministry at Jesus's death. The two stories included in this pericope show us two individuals who "know" Jesus and his abundant power. They don't fall into the trap of being unaware of who and what Jesus was. It wasn't a secret for them. Both the woman with the issue of blood and Jairus had heard stories about Jesus and came to receive his healing power. Jairus wants Jesus to come heal his sick daughter; he wants it so badly that he searches out a healer. Despite a pause in the action as Jesus heals the woman, Jairus's daughter is transformed from death to life. The woman with the issue of blood wants an end to her bleeding and her isolation from society due to her twelve years of hemorrhaging. She wants it so badly that she risks everything to seek Jesus out. They both believed in the power of Jesus. But knowing that something may be true is one thing. "Knowing" it to be an accessible truth to the core of your being, and then acting on that belief, is something entirely different. Jairus and the woman suffering from hemorrhages both knew and acted on their beliefs.

In the Gospel of Mark, Jesus is also often portrayed as having a problematic relationship with Jewish leadership. In this text, Jesus is both receptive and responsive to Jairus, who is a Jewish leader. Furthermore, the contrast of this "known" male and the unnamed woman is telling. In both instances there is a physical transformation: the daughter is brought back to life and the woman's body is cured. Jesus himself even feels the flow of energy leaving his body. The reality of the woman with the twelve-year bleeding condition is stunning. She heard about Jesus, she went to see and hear him, she approached him in a crowd, she touched his cloak, and as she walked away, Jesus called out to her—and she responded. She could have slipped out through the crowd, but she revealed herself to him. She came back out of fear, but despite that, she did return. Jesus commended her for her faith, and it was her faith that made her well. The lessons of this text are numerable and it's one of the reasons I love this text.

When Jesus taught, people listened, and stories of his work were spreading. Some heard a prophet, some heard a healer, some heard a teacher, and some heard a threat. Perspective is everything. Jairus and the woman with the hemorrhage heard in the stories of Jesus's teaching and healing a possibility for hope, healing, and health for themselves and those whom they loved. What an amazing gift. Hope has that kind of impact on us; it has the ability to transform us.

Sermon Extras

Seeking Holiness

It can be daunting to take time to meditate and reflect on the ways we are in need of healing. There are so many concerns and so many issues that we suffer from; each family has its issues, many of which can keep them up at night. The issue of suffering is complicated and confusing. If we can get past the need to blame or explain and live into the truth that our lives are a blessed gift, then we can bring a level of peace to our minds and hearts. Spending time in meditation and listening to these texts can be a powerful experience.

Encourage your people to embrace these stories as a prayer practice. Encourage your people to imagine the ways God has "healed" them of, or transformed them from, their pain, prejudices, insecurities, or needs. This has already happened for most of us in both big and small ways. We may not be fully aware of these transformations, but they are there. If we have the faith of Jairus and of the woman with the issue of blood, then transformations can happen. Encourage your people to pray for others in need, to live out their faith in positive and active ways, and to be present with those still longing for an end to their suffering. You can teach centering prayers both to children and to adults, helping them focus on this idea.

Worship Helps

Gathering Prayer

Lord, focus our thoughts on the ways we can come to know you and feel your presence in our lives. Focus our minds on the ways we can hear the stories of Jesus once again, and in new ways. Focus our prayers on the ways our lives are transformed by the power of Jesus. Focus our words and our ways on you, O Lord. Amen.

Call to Worship

We come into worship with baggage.
We come with wounds and suffering.
God knows the size and color of our baggage.
God knows the cause of our pain and concerns.
Into these moments, Jesus transforms our lives.
Into this place, Jesus meets us in our needs.
ALL: Holy One, lead us to trust in you, now and always. Amen.

Offering Invitation

Holy and Loving God, we offer you these gifts for the church and for the world. We offer our lives as your followers to impact others by living our faith. All things come from you and we give you thanks. Today we return our gifts to you. Bless them to do your will in the world. Amen.

Sending Forth

Send us forth in love and grace to serve the Lord. Send us with thanksgiving on our lips. Send us with kindness in our hearts. Send us to live a life of prayer in our thoughts and deeds. Amen.

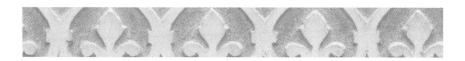

July 4, 2021–Sixth Sunday after Pentecost

2 Samuel 5:1-5, 9-10 or Ezekiel 2:1-5; Psalm 48 or Psalm 123;
2 Corinthians 12:2-10; Mark 6:1-13

Javier A. Viera

Preaching Theme

Maya Angelou once wrote about history, saying that it "cannot be unlived but, if faced with courage, need not be lived again."[1]

What a hopeful sentiment. It is worth it to personally explore the implications of this truth, but it's also an appropriate truth to be reminded of during this weekend observance of our nation's freedom. It's a hopeful truth for a people to know that they are not bound to repeat the sins of their forebears. It's hopeful for a people to consider the possibility of a future that can, in fact, be different. I think it is safe to say that this is a lesson this nation has learned well, albeit through wrenching, painful, shameful periods of its history.

Don't lose sight of the fact that Ms. Angelou was born into a society where she was not fully free, where she was relegated to an inferior status because of her race and gender. Yet, during her lifetime she went from the segregated confinement of a pre–civil rights America to an America in which someone much like her was elected to the nation's highest office. Getting to that historical point required traveling on a long, wrenching, painful road, but because it was faced with courage, we now live in a country that continues to overcome its past (or better said, we are a people who continue to overcome our past). However, there is much in our national discourse to suggest that some of the honest, hard work that was done in order not to keep repeating a shameful past is being undone. It's time for this nation to once again take collective stock of what we value and what we stand for, and we should not shy away from this in our preaching this Sunday.

It is equally important to be reminded of this on an individual level as well. Maya Angelou knew well that she was not confined to the painful periods of her personal history. The apostle Paul, when grappling with what he called his "thorn in the flesh"—that personal demon that tormented him, tempted him, weighed on him, shamed him—faced it with courage and truthfulness, and learned that, in doing so, he became stronger as a result of his weakness (**2 Cor 12:7** KJV). "Whenever I am weak, then I am strong," he said (2 Cor 12:10 NRSV). Ernest Hemingway expressed a similar idea in this way: "The world breaks everyone and afterward many are strong at the broken places."[2]

That's what we should be considering this morning. What would it mean for you to be strong in the broken places? What would it mean for you to be free of the thorn in your flesh, to be bigger than the personal demon that has haunted you for too long? These are questions of spiritual freedom, and today our lessons confront us with a stark choice: will you be free or not?

In our Gospel lesson for today, don't you imagine that Jesus was devastated when he went home to his synagogue, his friends, and his relatives in his hometown, only to be received so poorly? But he refused to be confined by a past others wanted to chain him to. It turns out that Jesus wasn't simply the little boy they remember; he was more than just a carpenter, more than just Joseph's and Mary's boy, and more than just a sibling. He refused to let those most familiar with him, perhaps even closest to him, define him and confine him to a smaller version of himself. He chose to be free of that, and it was painful, yet liberating at the same time. It was a turning point in his maturity.

Paul also refused to let his burden define him. In a moment of spiritual clarity and maturity, he wrote "whenever I am weak, then I am strong." He could say this because he knew to trust the God, who in Paul's moments of weakness, said to him, "My grace is sufficient for you, for power is made perfect in weakness" (2 Cor 12:9 NRSV). This is a tough message for us to accept personally, and much tougher to accept as a nation. Yet, that is the gospel truth and we proclaim it unapologetically because we know it is our only hopeful way forward.

Sermon Extras

Seeking Holiness

Some of our parishioners will come to church today in the midst of a personal crisis or deep struggle. Others will come clinging to their thorns or personal demons. Still others will come during a moment of personal confusion or during what feels like a moment in which they must make a monumental choice. Some will come hoping to find some wisdom or direction and hoping the preacher will speak a word that will help them deal with that thorn in their flesh. Consider ending your sermon, or your service, with a collective exercise of spiritual reflection, discipline, and prayer. Ask your congregants to name, in their minds and hearts, that thorn in their flesh that they cannot find freedom from: depression, addiction, confusion, fear, doubt, and so on. Once they have identified what it is for them, as a congregation pray or say together: "You no longer have power over me. God's grace is sufficient for me." Repeat that phrase several times together, and encourage them to make it their mantra for the week, and encourage them to speak with you or someone in the congregation who will encourage and support them in prayer about this "thorn" throughout the week and in the ensuing weeks. You might also consider doing this same exercise for the nation. Have them name what they believe is our nation's "thorn in the flesh" and perform the same spiritual exercise for our nation throughout the week.

Worship Helps

Gathering Prayer

Lord, there is much in our past of which we are proud and in which we find hope for the future. Yet, there is also much in our past that pains us, shames us, and that we know requires us to attempt to make right. Give us the strength and courage, personally and as a nation, to do the work that is before us to make our nation a beacon of hope, a land of true liberty and justice, and a place of welcome and succor for all who seek peace. Amen.

Call to Worship

Blessed is the nation whose God is the Lord, and the people whom God has chosen as a heritage.
Righteousness exalts a nation; justice is God's will made known.
You shall bless the Lord your God for the good land you have been given.
Our souls wait for the Lord; God is our help and shield.
Let us worship God.

July 11, 2021–Seventh Sunday after Pentecost

*2 Samuel 6:1-5, 12b-19 or Amos 7:7-15; Psalm 24 or Psalm 85:8-13;
Ephesians 1:3-14; Mark 6:14-29*

Laurie K. Zelman

Preaching Theme

Amos sees a vision, which the Lord has given him, and Amos knows he has been given a mission to communicate this vision to the people. A plumb line is a string with a precisely crafted weight on one end. On building guru Bob Vila's website, I found this description of a plumb line: "The plumb bob or plumb line employs the law of gravity to establish what is 'plumb' (that is, what is exactly vertical, or true)."[3] Vila describes the plumb line as an ancient builder's tool, which is thought to have been used in building the Egyptian pyramids and is still used today. Vila notes that one can use a plumb line to gauge the soundness of structures from a distance, as well as close up. When used, the plumb line is suspended from the top on a nail or other fixed point, and it is allowed to swing freely until it comes to a rest; in this way, the device reveals what is straight, sound, and true.

Amos stirs up resentment and fear as he articulates his vision that the governing body of the land is "out of true." The people are out of alignment with God, and God does not condone the power structure that includes the king and the religious authorities. The king tries to shut down the criticism, and the priests tell Amos to get out of town. Amos's response is that he is not a pundit. Amos has street cred; he is a working man, a blue-collar guy. In fact, his trade is to snip and prune trees to make them fruitful. Moreover, God has given him the responsibility to speak the vision he was given. The people are out of alignment and need to straighten up. Amos can use his practical skills to prune what is false and unproductive, both in the government and in the temple's structure.

Amos's vision highlights a basic tenet of Judeo-Christian faith: the truth is important to God. Being out of alignment with the truth will provoke God's rejection. Postmodern thinkers have long pointed out that, in our time, there is no capital-T truth that holds true for everyone, revealing that we all read scripture through the lens of culture and experience. Opinions about how we (and, perhaps, especially our opinions about how others) can live out the life of a true believer swing wildly between differing interpretations. We can even come to very different practical applications when looking to the same scriptures for guidance. How, then, do we find the truth that will align us with God's favor?

The plumb line hangs from a fixed point. For Christians, that fixed point must be Jesus. Jesus's actions reveal that he reaches over and beyond cultural barriers to call people to forgiveness, acceptance, and transformation. Jesus's teaching gives us a fixed reference from which to interpret the whole of the law: *"You must love the Lord your God with all your heart, with all your being, with all your strength, and with all your mind, and love your neighbor as yourself"* (**Luke 10:27**).

Sermon Extras

Engaging Kids

A plumb bob can be borrowed or purchased; one can be found for under $10 on the internet. To demonstrate the use of the plumb line, the leader can hold a plumb line while children watch for it to come to a rest. Then, the children can see if they can sight whether various walls in the church are straight. (The trustees may find some new recruits this way.) Next, kids can take turns to see how straight they can stand up or sit up next to the plumb line. The benefits of standing or sitting straight, as though we have a plumb line inside of us, can be explored with the kids. For example, we can breathe better, our muscles are more comfortable, we don't get tense, and we can face life's challenges openly and bravely. From there, exploring what it means to be in alignment with God's will is a natural step. How does God want us to line up with God's plan for us?

Sometimes the advice to pastors is to keep tight control of the children's time; it can be a risk asking children what they really think. However, children do have opinions and ideas, and they can surprise you with their insights. I recommend allowing children to respond naturally to questions rather than eliciting pre-programmed "right" answers; passing the microphone to them is a small risk to take when the benefit comes in the form of real engagement and in nurturing the beginnings of their theological thinking. For this scripture, gently guiding children toward the themes of telling the truth, engaging in study, praying and worshiping, practicing forgiveness, loving our neighbors, loving God, and even loving the unlovable, can be brought out through questioning and listening to their responses.

Worship Helps

Gathering Prayer

We enter your holy place, O God, seeking to worship you in truth. Help us to know your will for us. Give us courage to open our hearts and lives to you, as we sing and speak and hear your word. Amen.

Call to Worship

God of peace, fill our hearts.
We welcome your peace, O God.
God of life, make us lively in worship.
We long to live in you, O Christ.
God of righteousness, walk before us.
Holy Spirit, lead us in your ways.

Prayer of Confession

O God, we want to come into your presence as honest and loving people. But we swing back and forth on opinions. We find it easy to take ourselves more seriously than we take you. Forgive us, merciful God. Examine our hearts and minds and show us where we fall short of your truth. Show us where our thoughts need to be pruned, our attitudes brought into the light of your love. Show us our neighbors, and help us to respond to their needs, becoming your hands and your heart in the world.

Assurance

Hear the good news: The God of compassion knows where we are out of balance and will bring us into alignment through God's transforming love.

Sending Forth

Align yourself with God, take the truth of God's love from this place out into the world.

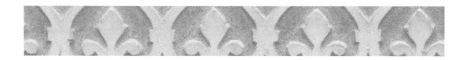

July 18, 2021–Eighth Sunday after Pentecost

2 Samuel 7:1-14a or Jeremiah 23:1-6; Psalm 89:20-37 or Psalm 23; Ephesians 2:11-22; Mark 6:30-34, 53-56

Lydia Muñoz

Preaching Theme

If you were to ask your congregation by a show of hands how many people have grown up with someone having a print of *The Lord is My Shepherd* by Warner Sallman, then I'm sure you would see plenty of hands in the air. As soon as you see the painting, you will recognize it because it's the one in which a blond-haired, blue-eyed Jesus guides his sheep through a backdrop of what might look like Scotland, rather than any place in the Middle East. In his arms he carries a soft, young sheep, and he is surrounded by white, fluffy sheep, with one black sheep walking behind him. It's a classic painting in every Sunday school or pastor's study, especially if your congregation dates from the 1940s or 1950s. This is the Shepherd whom we all see and relate to. He is kind and gentle, tall and—well, perfect. But he is not the kind of Shepherd who responds to David's seemingly kind gesture to build God a dwelling place. This Shepherd talks back and has something to say about David's grand idea. This Shepherd just isn't having it.

"Throughout all my travels with Israel, did I ever ask any of its leaders to build me a cedar temple?" (**2 Sam 7:7**, paraphrased).

In fact, God reminds David that God has been sojourning with Israel and has been most content to travel in a tent and a ready-made dwelling. This gives the impression that God has always been ready to pick up and move whenever it was needed, so much so that, perhaps, we get a glimpse of something incredible here: God is an immigrant.

God moves and travels, changes and adapts, just like our immigrant sisters and brothers do in order to build a better life for themselves. The identity of the Holy One with the migrant is deeply embedded in scripture and is one worthy of exploring during this time in our world. Just when the people of Israel thought they had things worked out, that they had figured out where and how to be God's people, God reminded them again that God can be contained neither by brick and mortar nor by any of our plans of grandeur. God is beyond all our trappings and our borders; God wants us to move with God wherever the Spirit leads.

Is that possible for us to do? Are we so wedded to our buildings, our structures, our own plans that we just might be too immobile for the Spirit to have room to do its work? Are we so settled that we are too afraid to venture to see what's next? Is it indeed easier for God to fit into our structures and plans than for us to be changed by God's?

This is the great question: Which is better: an immigrant church or a stable one that is part of an institution? What do we lose or gain in either one? Or is it possible that it's both-and? Are we able to reap the benefits of both?

These are good questions to explore with your congregation. If God is the Shepherd, are we really willing to be the sheep?

Sermon Extras

Seeking Holiness

Several years ago, I read an old book that a colleague gave to me called *A Shepherd Looks at Psalm 23*, written by Phillip Keller. Keller was born in East Africa and developed a love for the outdoors and the study of agronomy. He also lived among sheep and shepherds in British Columbia and observed their work. From these experiences, he has written a beautifully detailed description of his observation as it pertains to **Psalm 23**.

One of his descriptions is the process of cleaning a sheep's eyes and nose with oil in order to get out any obstruction or bugs that have been accumulating there. He's actually pretty raw in his description of this very necessary care for sheep by the shepherd, and it gives us a better picture of what the author of Psalm 23 might be referring to when the author writes, "you anoint my head with oil, my cup overflows" (v. 5 NRSV). Keller shares that although, even if this process is as unpleasant as it might seem, if it is not done, then the sheep could go blind, or try to hurt themselves because the gnats get into their ears so badly that they try to shake them off by hitting themselves against rocks, which may result in the sheep being injured.[4]

This is a great detail to know because it gives us a way to picture what the Spirit might have to do with us so that we can see and hear God's voice and call clearly. You might even want to pass around some small bowls of oil for people to feel with their hands as you preach about this very point. Using all the senses in preaching is a gift because there are a variety of learners within any given congregation.

Engaging Kids

A great way to talk about this passage with children is to compare the Good Shepherd with taking care of a pet. Perhaps some of the children can share about their pets, such as their pets' names and how they care for their pets.

A good pet owner provides food, water, shelter, and warmth and spends time with the pet. Now, every parent knows that we are truly the pets' caretakers; most of the time we are the ones who really take care of our children's pets, but they can still relate to this kind of care.

Share how the ultimate caregiver, God as the Good Shepherd, knows truly how to care for us and that's why, in ancient times, people compared God to a shepherd who took care of God's sheep in the field.

Perhaps you can bring a picture of a pet you have so that they can see how you take care of animals as well. You can explain where the name *pastor* comes from, which is a great way to make a connection. Just remember not to set yourself up to perfect status.

Worship Helps

A Prayer of Confession (Based on Psalm 23)

The Lord is my shepherd.
> But why do I feel like I am lacking?

My Shepherd leads me to grassy meadows and peaceful waters.
> But why do I not feel restful?

My Shepherd guides me through good paths.
> But why do I insist on taking my own way?

It is you who walks with me in the darkest of valleys.
It is you who protects me with your rod and your staff, even when I don't want it.
> Why does my heart feel fear?

My Shepherd pours oil over me to refresh my soul and showers me with an abundance of life.
> Why do I allow my soul to become clouded by the weight of the world
> until I feel close to death?

> [Silent confession.]

Words of Pardon and Assurance

Yet your goodness and mercy persistently follow me all the days of my life, they never let me go.
Even in my weakness, you welcome me into your house as your family forever.
> Nothing will ever change that for all my days.

July 25, 2021–Ninth Sunday after Pentecost

2 Samuel 11:1-15 or 2 Kings 4:42-44; Psalm 14 or Psalm 145:10-18; Ephesians 3:14-21; John 6:1-21

Harriett Olson

Preaching Theme

One lens through which to read today's texts would be to look at the use or abuse of power. For example, King David abused his power. Bathsheba did not relinquish hers, but she demanded that David respond by notifying him that she was pregnant. The psalmist sees God's power used for good and sees the power of the unjust being insufficient to protect them. Jesus exercises power but refuses to be pulled into the realm of political power. Power itself is morally neutral in these passages, but the uses of power are not. Those who have power must use it righteously, honoring others, looking out for others' needs, and fulfilling their own callings. Indeed, Paul prays that the members of the church at Ephesus will have the power to grasp love's vast scope. What if we were animated by the power of our vision of God's love—for each of us and all of us, no matter what nation or ethnic group?

Another lens through which to preach would be to focus on the theme of abundance. While lifting up God's power and care for the people, the psalmist gives voice to the hope (perhaps the longing) of the people for food "at the right time" and that the desires of every living thing (not just the people) would be satisfied (**Ps 145:15-16**). We would do well to join in this hope today, a time in which the minimum wage is not a living wage and support for the poor is undermined for tax cuts for the wealthy. Contrast this with Jesus's feeding of five thousand people on "the other side" of the Sea of Galilee (**John 6:1** NRSV). It is worth noting that this story takes place in the area of the Decapolis, a Greek region, which is beyond the borders of Herod's rule. Some of the people hearing the message had followed Jesus, but no doubt some were non-Jews. Jesus fed them all until they were satisfied (just as Paul longs for all people to come to the fullness of God in our **Ephesians** passage).

The disciples did not see abundance. In John's version of the story, Jesus initiates the conversation and asks how the people are to be fed. Certainly, we can identify with the disciples. Philip is stuck on the enormity of the challenge. How often is this true for us? Andrew identifies some possible resources (five barley loaves and two fish) but immediately diminishes their capacity to meet the challenge. Likewise, we might also be tempted to ask, "But what can one person do?" or "How could the action of our congregation make any difference?" Jesus, however, organizes the people and blesses and breaks the bread, distributing them until all have eaten their fill, and then collects the leftovers. May we never fail to offer ourselves or our substance because of our sense of inadequacy.

John says that Jesus distributed the bread and fish and you may see in this Jesus's giving himself to us and for us, with plenty to go around and plenty to spare for those not already gathered. This interpretation is hinted at through the reference to the imminent Passover season, in which the people would remember their ancestors being spared due to the blood spread over the doorways of their homes in Egypt. Jesus shelters and feeds us, offering to fill our spiritual yearning, connecting again to Paul's prayer that the believers would be strengthened "from the riches of [Christ's] glory through the Spirit" (Eph 3:16). And that they grasp love's expansiveness, knowing Christ's love and being "filled entirely with the fullness of God" (Eph 3:18-19).

As we reach out to grasp this spiritual abundance that God can provide, how can you imagine that we might demonstrate that we are full of the fullness of God? Would we appreciate our own gifts and those of others more joyfully? Would we initiate responses to others' needs in the confidence that God "is able to do far beyond all that we could ask or imagine" (Eph 3:20)?

Worship Helps

Gathering Prayer

Gracious God, we come together as your people to marvel at your amazing gifts to us—gifts of strength, gifts of challenge, gifts of faith, gifts of community, and, most of all, the gift of new life in Jesus Christ. Help us to open our hearts to hear your word to us today, that we may be filled with your fullness and be faithful in responding to the needs of others.

Offertory Prayer

All things come from you, loving God, and you entrust them to us for our needs and enjoyment, and for the needs and enjoyment of others. May the gifts that we bring this day, and the service that we offer, be pleasing in your sight as we seek to know and to show the width and length, height and depth of your love, through the power of the Holy Spirit. Amen.

August 1, 2021–Tenth Sunday after Pentecost

2 Samuel 11:26–12:13a or Exodus 16:2-4, 9-15; Psalm 51:1-12 or Psalm 78:23-29; Ephesians 4:1-16; John 6:24-35

Sudarshana Devadhar

Preaching Theme

Paul's message to the Christians in Ephesus, found in today's lectionary reading, is similar to his message to the Corinthian church, which was divided and caught up in unhelpful debates about which gifts were more important than others. These churches, like many of the churches we know, experienced unhealthy competition, divisions, and conflict. Paul writes to the Ephesians from his prison cell at a time of unhealthy conduct among the members of the faith community. He encourages them "to live as people worthy of the call" (**Eph 4:1**) they received from God. He then goes on to spell that out: he speaks about the unity of the body of Christ and the variety of gifts God has bestowed upon each one. The lectionary passage concludes with Paul's contrasting description of how they are *not to act* (as infants tossed and blown around) with how they *should live* (as those growing in every way into Christ).

The twenty-first-century church shares some commonalities with the early church in spite of the difference in time and context. The Pentecost season affords us the opportunity to teach, as well as to preach, and the lectionary text for this Sunday from Ephesians provides several possibilities.

For example, let us center in on the second verse: "Conduct yourselves with all humility, gentleness, and patience. Accept each other with love." What does it mean to conduct oneself with humility, gentleness, and patience in a world in which humility is often viewed as a weakness? What does gentleness look like when there is a push to win, win, win? What does patience look like when everyone is looking for instant gratification? What does acceptance of our enemies and strangers look like in a divided world? What is the mark of genuine Christian love? Jesus demonstrated love through his life, ministry, death, and resurrection. We have been called and given gifts to be the body of Christ. A sermon could focus on the radical invitation to conduct our lives, individually and corporately, in the way that Paul describes.

Another possibility comes from the fifth and sixth verses. The apostle Paul wrote, "There is one Lord, one faith, one baptism, and one God and Father of all, who is over all, through all, and in all." Even, and perhaps especially, within the church, it is important to exegete "one Lord" and "lordship of Jesus Christ" and discuss the context in which Paul wrote these words. Confusion about "Jesus as Lord" has been used against persons of other faiths and has warped the church's understanding of evangelism. A sermon focused on the latter would be a helpful antidote to the narrow interpretations that have damaged interfaith relationships. Another approach to a sermon based on this verse would be to ask what the phrase "There is one Lord" means for the way Christians spend their time, use their money, focus their attention, and exercise their civic responsibility—and privilege—to vote? To what other "gods" have Christians pledged allegiance? How can Christians speak about "one Lord, one faith, one baptism, one God" and relate to and converse with people of other faiths, as well as with people who profess no faith?

A third option can be found in the eleventh and twelfth verses. Here, Paul wrote, "He gave some apostles, some prophets, some evangelists, and some pastors and teachers. His purpose was to equip God's people for the work of serving and building up the body of Christ." One may develop a sermon on Christian discipleship focused on discovering, developing, and employing spiritual gifts in building up the body of Christ. The nominations and leadership committees are key in determining how well gifts and services are developed and employed for the ministry of the laity. The committee plays a key role in identifying and calling forth the spiritual gifts of others for service in the church and in the world.

Sermon Extras

Dismantling Oppression

Worshippers might be encouraged to visit other congregations, both churches of other denominations and also Jewish synagogues, Islamic mosques, Sikh gurdwaras, Hindu temples, and so on in order to gain inspiration and an understanding about how to participate and cooperate with people of other denominations and faiths, and also about how to address the injustices done to the children of the one God who created us all.

Worship Helps

Gathering Prayer

Spirit of the living God, fall afresh upon us. Make us worthy of the calling we have received from you. Teach us to conduct ourselves with humility, gentleness, and patience. Convert our judgment to acceptance. Give us courage to preserve the unity of the Spirit with the bond of peace. Blow upon us new winds of the Spirit. Send your fire to refine, consume, and transform. We pray in Christ's holy name. Amen.

Call to Worship (Based on Psalm 51:10, 11)

Create a clean heart for me, God;
put a new, faithful spirit deep inside me!
Please don't throw me out of your presence;
please don't take your Holy Spirit away from me.

Benediction

May the power of the Holy Spirit equip us for the work of serving and building up the body of Christ.
May the grace of Christ teach us to speak the truth with love.
May the love of God mature and grow in us until the body builds itself up with love and each one does their part.
The grace of our Lord Jesus Christ, the love of God, and the power of the Holy Spirit be with you and remain with you always. Amen.

August 8, 2021–Eleventh Sunday after Pentecost

2 Samuel 18:5-9, 15, 31-33 or 1 Kings 19:4-8; Psalm 130 or Psalm 34:1-8; Ephesians 4:25–5:2; John 6:35, 41-51

James F. McIntire

Focusing Prayer

God, in teaching me to own my own bitterness and anger, teach me also to accept the difficulty in doing so. Let my words and my life be examples of putting them aside in favor of imitating the Christ. Amen.

Preaching Theme

Fred Craddock's sermon "Praying Through Clenched Teeth" begins with these words:

> I am going to say a word and the moment I say the word I want you to see a face, to recall a face and a name, someone who comes to your mind when I say the word. Are you ready? The word is *bitter.* Bitter. Do you see a face? I see a face.[1]

He then continues in classic Craddock-storytelling-mode, describing several bitter faces and the situations that caused the bitterness until his illustration ends with:

> Will you look at one other face? His name is Saul. Saul of Tarsus.[2]

Paul a bitter man? Was he bitter because he felt like he was a man of status—a Roman citizen, a leader in his community, a teacher of the right way—who was forced to persecute this low-life Christian sect within Judaism? Was he bitter because he thought of himself as a man of virtue, a strict follower of the law, and an observant Jew, therefore despising anyone he thought had strayed from God's commanded law—those who believed the stories of Jesus-the-law-beaker and still followed him, Jesus who maybe claimed messiahship, who healed on the Sabbath, who plucked grain from the fields on the Sabbath, who ate with sinners, and who defiled God's very being?

Was Paul bitter because he thought he was living right, obeying God, following the commandments to the letter of the law when God literally knocks him to the ground, blinds him, and turns his life-course a completely different direction? Was Paul a bitter man because after his epiphany and becoming a follower of the same Jesus whose followers he had hated, he found that they weren't too interested in what he had to say? He taught them all he knew—yet they strayed and did whatever they wanted anyway—mismanaging their money; acting as though it were Jews versus Gentiles; bickering and quarreling; engaging in conflicts within and fighting without; being at peace and war; eating food that wasn't theirs; arguing over who is the greatest teacher among them; engaging in sex or abstinence; promoting slavery or equality; performing baptism and circumcision; engaging in acts of anger, backbiting, backsliding, debauchery, factions, arguments, envy, boasting, arrogance, and rudeness. (Good thing Christians aren't like *that* anymore, right?!?)

In this letter to the Ephesians, which was probably not composed by Paul but by one of his students, anger and deceit within the fellowship had become serious concerns (**Eph 4:25-27**). People were taking advantage of one another and some may have been only partially reformed thieves (v. 28). He knew that when people are riled up about issues, they often criticize and condemn one another mercilessly. Paul instructs, "Don't let any foul words come out of your mouth" (v. 29).

Bitterness. Paul knew it; Paul must have had it deep within himself. His thorn in the flesh perhaps? Or was it that thorn that deepened his bitterness—toward God, toward the Christian communities, toward himself? Bitterness. "It's been my experience," said Abraham Lincoln, "that people with no vices have very few virtues." Paul knew bitterness because he lived bitterness. Paul could counsel his students about bitterness because he had tried to control his own bitterness.

"Imitate God like dearly loved children. Live your life with love, following the example of Christ, who loved us and gave himself for us" (Eph 5:1-2). God knows it's not easy, but it's the God-path and the letter suggests some examples of what such imitation might mean: "*Be angry without sinning.* Don't let the sun set on your anger. Don't provide an opportunity for the devil.... Only say what is helpful when it is needed for building up the community so that it benefits those who hear what you say.... Put aside all bitterness, losing your temper, anger, shouting, and slander, along with every other evil. Be kind, compassionate, and forgiving to each other, in the same way God forgave you in Christ" (Eph 4:26-32).

Good words or bad words; evil words or kind words; critical words or loving words; truthful words or deceptive words. Either of those juxtaposed words will get planted, take root, grow, and become reality in someone's life. Choose carefully which words you'll use; let the words of your mouth carry the message of your God (preachers especially take note).

God's words. Our words. They all mean something. They all create something. They create something between us. Move beyond words of bitterness and anger and resentment; use words wisely in the knowledge that they can carry hurt as well as beauty. Paul knew for himself that he had to "put aside all bitterness" and move beyond anger, and he tried to get the early Christian communities to understand this and live this: "Don't let any foul words come out of your mouth."

But we just don't get it, do we?

Depending on context, the sermon might fill out more of Dr. Craddock's illustration of bitterness. After several descriptions, he writes:

> Do you see a face? A young minister in a small town in a cracker box of a house they call a parsonage. He lives there with his wife and small child. It's Saturday morning. There is a knock at the door; he answers and there standing before him on the porch is the chairman of his church board, who is also the president of the local bank, and also the owner of most of the land roundabout. The man has in his hands a small television. It's an old television, small screen, black and white. It's badly scarred and one of the knobs is off. He says, "My wife and I got one of those new 44-inch color sets but they didn't want to take this one on a trade, so I just said to myself, 'We will just give it to the minister. That's probably the reason our ministers don't stay any longer than they do. We don't do enough nice things for them.'"
>
> The young minister looks up, tries to smile and say thanks, but I want you to see his face. Bitter.[3]

Even if this is not used for your sermon, you might "enjoy" that story for yourself!

Sermon Extras

Seeking Holiness

A sermon on this text might invite the congregation to share words before or after the "bitterness" illustration. You might ask: What are people bitter about in their lives? What in the community makes people angry? Has there been an incident in which you've told a nontruth to another who is "part of the same body"? When is a moment you have used words that were not helpful for building up the community? Was there a time when you had been tempted to use foul words—not necessarily restricted to cursing?

Those are risky questions to ask, so it might be good to follow the old adage, "Never ask questions you aren't ready to hear the answers to." Or, "Never ask a question unless you already know the answer." A safer approach might be to share your own personal answers to some of those questions, or to solicit anonymous answers prior to preaching.

Use those words to play with the themes of bitterness, anger, helpful ways of building of the community, and so on.

Worship Helps

Call to Worship (Based on Psalm 34:1-8)

Let us bless God at all times.
Even when I don't feel like it?
Let us praise God,
let my suffering listen.
Magnify God with me!
I sought out God. Was there an answer?
God delivers us from fear.
At times I still fear.
God saves.
So, in that promise we cry out, "Save me, O God."
And God listened.
Taste and see how good God is!

Offering Prayer (Based on John 6:35, 41-51)

From the One who is "the bread of life,"
From the One who will never let us go hungry,
From the One who will never let us be thirsty;
we have received bread from heaven.
From that which we have received,
freely now we give
> *that hunger and thirst*
> *may be sated and quenched,*
By the very same One,
and by our dedication this day.
Amen.

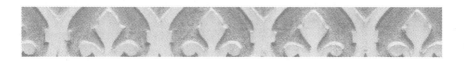

August 15, 2021–Twelfth Sunday after Pentecost

1 Kings 2:10-12, 3:3-14 or Proverbs 9:1-6; Psalm 111 or Psalm 34:9-14; Ephesians 5:15-20; John 6:51-58

Drew A. Dyson

Preaching Theme

Every Sunday morning, before leaving for church, my mother would set the table for Sunday dinner with at least three extra place settings for would-be guests. In my curiosity, I once asked why she would set such a fancy table when she didn't even know who would be joining us for dinner. "It doesn't matter," she replied, "whoever comes is our guest and will be received with hospitality and love."

By mid-afternoon on Sunday, every seat at the table would be filled. Maybe it would be the resident from the nursing home who hadn't had a visitor in months, or the visitor at church with whom Mom had connected during the passing of the peace, or the college student who looked eager for a home-cooked meal, or the grieving, recent widow. "Whoever comes" was received with love. And they got a great meal as well.

In the Gospel reading for today, there is power in Jesus's self-identification as the bread of life. Jesus understands that the offering of his life, the body and blood of Christ, is nothing less than the gift of salvation and eternal life. The meal that was offered was incomparable. The invitation, however, is what stands out.

As we read in **John**: "Whoever eats...will live forever"; "Those who eat...have eternal life"; "Those who eat...abide in me and I in them"; and "The one who eats...will live forever" (6:51-58 NRSV). Do you hear the power in the invitation? "Whoever comes...will be received with hospitality and love." Jesus's invitation to partake of this life-giving meal is an invitation to all of humanity. It crosses every boundary constructed by human hands.

Everyone, and anyone, is invited to partake in this sacred meal. How will you respond? And will your invitation be as generous? Who comes to your table? Who is invited? What are the boundaries that need to be removed in order to authentically reflect the unmatchable, unbounded gift of grace?

Sermon Extras

Engaging Kids

Use the children's time to share the power of an invitation that extends God's table to everyone. Set up an elaborate tea party or meal setting in the front of the sanctuary with enough "extras" to make it truly special. Invite the children to move through the congregation and "invite" a friend to join them at the table.

Doing Justice

The slower pace of summer is a good time for church leadership to reflect on the church's role in the community. How would your community define your church's invitation? Would it be perceived as generous and extravagant, offering the bread of life? Reflect with church leaders on the boundaries, real or perceived, that keep that from being the case. How will you address these concerns? Brainstorm together and develop a plan to extend the radical witness of God's unconditional love to your neighbors.

Worship Helps

Gathering Prayer

Gracious God, you have gathered us here as your family around your table to share in this sacred meal. We give thanks for the radical invitation that extends to all of your children. Help us be mindful of those who are not around the table—and help us be disciples committed to tearing down barriers of exclusion and injustice. As we worship together this morning, we dedicate ourselves to carrying your gracious invitation into the world. Give us courage to live out that ideal as we move forward in love and grace. Amen.

Call to Worship (Based on Psalm 111)

Give thanks to the Lord with your whole heart.
Great are the works of the Lord.
Full of honor and majesty are the works of God;
God's righteousness endures forever.
The Holy One sends redemption to the people;
holy and awesome is God's name.
The fear of the Lord is the beginning of wisdom.
ALL: Your praise endures forever.

Creative Worship Opportunity

Send invitations to your congregation and provide invitations that can be shared with neighbors in the community. Host a special mid-month communion service followed by a luncheon of fresh-baked bread and salads.

August 22, 2021–Thirteenth Sunday after Pentecost

1 Kings 8:(1, 6, 10-11) 22-30, 41-43 or Joshua 24:1-2a, 14-18; Psalm 84 or Psalm 34:15-22; Ephesians 6:10-20; John 6:56-69

Jennifer and Todd Pick

Preaching Theme

There are words in life that are difficult to hear, and sometimes even more impossible to say: "I'm sorry"; "I forgive you"; "I don't know"; "I love you"; "I was wrong"; and "Goodbye." Each of these phrases implies that we must strip away all the layers of protection we have built around our hearts over a lifetime of hurt. To say these words, we must break ourselves open and be vulnerable. Hard words and their consequences necessarily involve risk and faith. In the Gospel lesson for today, Jesus's followers encounter a difficult word while Jesus is teaching in the synagogue of Capernaum. The challenge to those early followers—and to us—presents this question: Are we willing to follow where this hard word leads, to risk safety and the offense of the cross to taste eternal life?

If you are following the lectionary, we are in the fifth (and final) week of the Bread of Life Discourse in **John**. These five weeks have probably stretched your imagination (as well as your patience), trying to come up with different things to say as variations on a similar theme for more than a month. But in this final section of text, we get to the crux of the matter. The first verse shocks the listener out of their complacency: "Whoever eats my flesh and drinks my blood remains in me and I in them" (John 6:56). Eating flesh and drinking blood will take most church people straight to the communion table with bread and cup. The first hearers of this "difficult word," however, might have tended to think that Jesus was talking about cannibalism and blood sacrifice. These are difficult words, indeed, for *any* audience, ancient or modern, who is not familiar with the ritual surrounding the Eucharist.

As we read in John 6:60, "Many of his disciples who heard this said, 'This message is harsh. Who can hear it?'" We must remember, when reading John's Gospel, the "disciples" and "the Twelve" are two different groups of people. A disciple is simply a follower of Jesus. This verse comes to us in a myriad of translations. In Greek, though, the actual word for *message* is *logos*—translated earlier in this Gospel as *Word* (with a capital *W*), as in: "In the beginning was the Word [*logos*], and the Word [*logos*] was with God and the Word [*logos*] was God" (**John 1:1**). What if these followers of

Jesus were looking at this man and saying, "This Word [*logos*] is hard. Who is able to hear it?" Jesus is a hard Word; he is hard to understand, hard to follow, and hard to comprehend. Perhaps the disciples thought that the way of Jesus would be easier; perhaps they thought that this path would be smoother than the other paths that they could have chosen. But here, at the last, Jesus offers himself as the bread of eternal life. For some, that bread turns out to be hard to swallow.

When Jesus saw the disciples complaining about this word that is hard, he asked them, "Does this Word scandalize you?" (John 6:61, author's translation). Our English translations soften the original Greek from *scandalize* to *offend*. The Johannine Jesus never wavers from what is difficult, and he calls his followers to do the same. Our scripture says that Jesus lost many of his disciples that day. The word was just too difficult. The way of the cross was just too scandalous—even if eternal life and resurrection were on the other side.

Jesus calls us and our congregations out too. Are we willing to risk the hard word for a chance at rising to new life? Are we willing to follow the living Word into places that we might not want to go, to have our hearts broken by the things that break Christ's heart? Are we willing to risk the wilderness for the promised land, or do we want to return to slavery? One thing is sure: we will never walk alone. Perhaps when we recognize that following the way of compassion and love leads us to a fuller life, then we can be able to respond as Peter did, "Lord, to whom can we go? You have the words of eternal life. We have come to believe and know that you are the Holy One of God" (John 6:68-69 NRSV).

Secondary Preaching Themes

If you have already abandoned the Bread of Life discourse, the other lectionary texts for this morning also hold wonderful homiletical treasures. In **1 Kings**, we catch Solomon in the middle of a very public prayer that speaks to the very character of God. How do your people make a place for God to dwell? Similarly, what is intriguing about the **Ephesians** passage is not the militaristic metaphor of the armor of God, but what comes afterward. The armor is just a means to an end—the end is having the confidence to tell the gospel story, to live into that story with integrity and not to compromise the eternal word for temporary comfort.

Worship Helps

Gathering Prayer

Bread of heaven, may we feast on your teachings so fully and absorb your words so completely that our hearts become like yours. Let your love live so fully in us until it becomes like our flesh and bone. Let your abundant life live so fully in us until we live your will and your way. Amen.

Call to Worship

If you are hungry for food or hungering for justice,
come and feast on the bread of heaven.
If you are thirsty for drink or thirsting for righteousness,
come and dine at the table that brings us into right relationship.
All who are hungry to share the presence of Christ,
come and share in the promise of life eternal.
Come, let grace find you. Come, let love fill you!
Come and worship! Come and dine!
Source of new life, come and feed us until we want no more!

Sending Forth

Here we go from the table again, full of invitation and blessing!
We are called to share Love's welcome!
Here we go from the table again, full of life and hope!
We are called to dance Love's promise!
Here we go from the table again, full of grace and mercy!
We are called to sing Love's story!
Full of Christ's abiding love, we are commissioned anew
to forgive as we have been forgiven,
to feed as we have been fed,
to love as we have been loved.
Here we go from the table again...
called and sent to live Love's way!

August 29, 2021–Fourteenth Sunday after Pentecost

Song of Solomon 2:8-13 or Deuteronomy 4:1-2, 6-9; Psalm 45:1-2, 6-9 or Psalm 15; James 1:17-27; Mark 7:1-8, 14-15, 21-23

Sheila M. Beckford

Preaching Theme

In 2014, to save money, the governmental authorities in Flint, Michigan, switched their water supply from the City of Detroit to the water from the Flint River. It was soon discovered that the water was contaminated. Due to being exposed to the contaminated water, people died of Legionnaires' disease and cancer; and children died of, and are still being affected by, lead poisoning. Despite the dangers, deaths, and cries from the affected community, authorities refused to address the poisoned water. In fact, they tried to cover it up for some time.

Initially, the investigation revealed those responsible for the negligence that caused the poisoning of the Flint, Michigan, residents. However, soon it was further revealed that greed and personal profit had affected their decisions around changing the water source.

If I were preaching this week, I would focus on the theme of spiritual contamination. Each text presents the idea of allowing different opinions, beliefs, and motives to contaminate God's gifts. Looking at the opening story of the Flint, Michigan, water crisis, on the surface, one may believe that it is antithetical to the theme. But if we look deeper, then we will see that the water contamination was the physical manifestation of a spiritual and moral contamination of those who were chosen to lead.

Spiritual contamination starts from the inside of human beings. It begins with our thoughts and our hearts (**Mark 7:21-23**). It then manifests itself through our actions. **James 1:22-26** goes even deeper into this idea. The writer of James contends that inaction defines *contamination*. One must not only say what they believe (as stated in Mark), but they must also live into their faith, propelling them to take action to protect the vulnerable. The James text clearly identifies the widow and the orphans, but the core teaching of the Bible extends far beyond these two particular groups to those who are marginalized or vulnerable.

James is a proponent for equity and equality. In **James 2:1-11**, the author explains that no follower of Christ should show favoritism to one group that has more than the other. Our laws today, spoken and unspoken, favor one group over the other. An examination of disproportionate jail sentences will show that one group is favored over another; we witness the manifestation of spiritual contamination frequently in our justice system. Looking at the disproportionate distribution of wages regarding men and women is another place in which we can see that there are cases of spiritual contamination.

We are reminded that the water we are to draw from is the uncontaminated word of God; it is the water that gives life. When we draw from other sources, we then draw contaminated water that no longer brings life, but brings death. James tells us that when we forget about the vulnerable, we live into the societal norms of contaminated waters. However, when we are both hearers and doers of the word, we purify or decontaminate those waters.

Sermon Extras

Engaging Kids

Here's an interactive way to engage children and adults:

On the altar or a table, set out pitchers of clean water. Also set out jars or bottles of different colored dyes; the bottles should be labeled with various ills afflicting the world, such as hunger, violence, war, loneliness, racism, and so on. Also, have a bottle ready that contains a mild solution of chlorine bleach, baking soda, and water (find instructions for this solution online).

Follow these instructions:

1. Slowly add drops of food coloring to some of the water while calling out the labels.

2. Select a group of children to receive the clean water. Also select a group to receive the dyed or dirty water.

3. Take out the bottle of bleach solution and add droplets to the dyed water.

4. Explain to the children: The droplets represent Jesus, who decontaminates our hearts to be those who work to bring hope to those who are marginalized. The one who looks at all people through the same lens and offers each person clean, purified, living water that gives us life is the giver of life.

Go out into the world, decontaminating the muddy waters with the power of Jesus. Spread the word of James that to be complicit is to be contaminated. The water of life is for all. Go and share this life-giving message to all whom you encounter.

Worship Helps

Gathering Prayer

We come into this place of worship to offer all of ourselves in praise. During this time of Pentecost, we continue to celebrate your power and our purpose as believers who both listen and respond to your call to justice. Gather us as one, we pray in Jesus's name. Amen.

Call to Worship

Lord, we lift our voices in song to worship you.
All good and perfect gifts are from you.
Lord, we offer ourselves to one another in the spirit of your love.
All good and perfect gift comes from you.
Lord, we are thankful for your grace.
Lord, you are majestic. We thank you for your perfect gifts of song, dance, poetry, and other expressions of love you have blessed us with. We use them to praise and worship you! Amen.

Prayer of Confession

We confess that we have not loved you with a pure heart. We acknowledge, Lord, that we too have contributed to the contamination of your loving waters. Forgive us for our complicity in muddying the waters of life. Help us to decontaminate our lives so that we can be both hearers and doers of justice for those who are considered the other.

September 5, 2021– Fifteenth Sunday after Pentecost

Proverbs 22:1-2, 8-9, 22-23 or Isaiah 35:4-7a; Psalm 125 or Psalm 146;
James 2:1-10 (11-13), 14-17; Mark 7:24-37

Laurie K. Zelman

Preaching Theme

It's a dog-eat-dog world, from social insects to birds to mammals. The term *pecking order* comes from the observation of flocks of chickens and literally describes how chickens make their way to the top in the coop. Competition and hierarchy are features built into the animal world. Renowned naturalist Jane Goodall observed and clarified the hierarchical world of chimpanzee behavior, where alpha males get the best food and the most chances to reproduce. The price for this exalted position is constant vigilance for usurpers, risk of injury, and high levels of stress hormones that suppress the immune system and promote inflammation.

Somehow, humanity seems to instinctively operate on similar dynamics. We humans are programmed to look for status and to look for our place within the groups we find ourselves. Not only that, but we seem to naturally and culturally orient ourselves to look up and to experience envy for those who are higher in the pecking order. We compare not only our material possessions but also our abilities, our talents, our accomplishments, and our blessings with those who look like they have been granted a bigger helping than we have. Mark Twain wrote, "Comparison is the death of joy." When we compare ourselves to others, we practically guarantee our own discontent. But when we refuse to play the comparison game and strive for gratitude for what we have, we claim the inheritance of contentment for what God gives.

The author of the letter of **James** calls Jesus's commandment to love our neighbor as ourselves the "royal law," and gives the faithful practical instruction about how to live into this fundamental tenet (2:8). Obedience to this law challenges not only our culture but also our hard wiring, bringing into question both ancient cultural assumptions and instinctive behavior. It's disturbing to note how apt James's words are for the world we live in more than two thousand years later. We can be slaves to status and the quest for power, we can focus on a quest for the technology, the car, the dress, or the address that connotes success. We humans still treat others according to how they fit into our notions of who's up and who's down.

James also calls the law of loving your neighbor "the law of freedom" (**1:25**). The ancient world was relentlessly hierarchical. The brilliance of the founders of the United States and other democracies was to weave God's "royal law" into founding documents so that the basic equality of constituents is encoded into the structure of society. Social mobility is a fruit of living into the freedom gained by attempts to live into the scriptural vision of God's reign on earth. In aligning ourselves with God's love for us and for our neighbor, we can consciously interrupt old instincts to uphold the hierarchy. We can do more, be better, and be agents of God's will on earth. When we look across at equals, not up and down at superiors and inferiors, we are creating space for freedom in Christ.

Sermon Extras

Seeking Holiness

Communities in many areas post signs that they are striving to be "stigma free," which typically refers to the stigma surrounding mental illness or addiction. The sting of stigma is often felt by individuals who have been diagnosed with psychiatric illness and substance use disorders. These devastating illnesses can impact, strain, and interrupt jobs and living situations, and destabilize relationships. And comparing life to what it was before an illness, or comparing oneself to those who don't have to deal with the same problems, is a constant temptation. In the Partial Care mental health program where I work, we recommend and teach ways that people can shift from comparing oneself to others and instead focus on healing from losses. Sometimes, we work with clients on keeping a gratitude journal. Choosing a time each day to write down large and small things one notices and is grateful for can be an aid to altering one's focus from what's missing to what blessings are present. Another technique that can be adopted is a shift in perspective called radical acceptance, which involves abstaining from investing energy in regret and anger about how things are, and just practicing acceptance of the difficulty and challenge of each day. This creates a freedom that can allow us to move toward being able to envision and initiate change. Both of these practices can be adopted as spiritual disciplines for anyone who is struggling with making comparisons between self and others.

Worship Helps

Gathering Prayer

You are the center, holy God. Your love is where we find balance, your word is where we find inspiration, your song is where our hearts sing. Bring us here and now into your holy presence, God of all, let us worship in the freedom that you bring to all souls. Amen.

Offering Invitation

As we are free to accept Christ's love, make us free also to give. Create generous hearts in us, so that the love of God may spread from this place to our neighbors around us and beyond that to our neighbors in the world community. Amen.

Prayer of Repentance

Our God, you are also God of others very different from us. We confess to you that there are times when we want to be better than, when we want to climb the ladder at the expense of others, when we take for granted and hoard your gifts, when we fail to realize that you want us to love others as you love them. Forgive us, show us your mercy, let our hearts break so that your love may enter and move through us. Amen.

Assurance

Christ meets us in our brokenness and leads us to transformation. Know the freedom of God's forgiveness and the power of God's love.

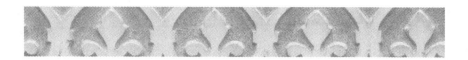

September 12, 2021– Sixteenth Sunday after Pentecost

Proverbs 1:20-33 or Isaiah 50:4-9a; Psalm 19 or Psalm 116:1-9 or Wisdom of Solomon 7:26–8:1; James 3:1-12; Mark 8:27-38

Kathleen Stone

Focusing Prayer

Oh, Lord, in all ways, help me to make the choices in my life that affirm life, and love, and heart. Do not let me be moved by fear, but help me make those decisions that best collaborate with the brilliant, generous light of your Holy Spirit, without whom I would surely be less. Amen.

Preaching Theme

Who do I say I am?

When Peter announced to that small band of followers that Jesus was, of course, the Messiah, that meant some things that our Christian tradition hasn't interpreted very well. We glibly say that Jesus is our Messiah. During the time of the Roman Empire, the common knowledge of the Jewish faith was that the Messiah would come to the Jewish people and would be the last great ruler on earth. As found in Daniel, the Messiah, the Son of Man, would be the one who would make all things right. Following his own declaration that Jesus was the Messiah, Jesus's dire prediction must have shocked Peter. If he claimed Jesus as the Jewish Messiah, that meant this victor would rise to ruling status by violently overthrowing the current regime while the heavens affirmed his rule. I can't even imagine Peter getting his head around what Jesus now said, that he would suffer and die. Peter must have been constantly wondering: "Is it now? Will the heavens open now so that Jesus would sit on the throne of David and all would finally be right?" When Jesus spoke these dire words, Peter must have been thinking: "Was Jesus just being cynical and losing faith?" And if he was, didn't that deserve a scolding? "How could you say such things, Jesus?!"

What was it like for Jesus to disappoint people by living into his authenticity, as God's true Son, rather than into the false images that people had of him—the false images that were full of the people's hopes to be saved in real time, in a real place of this Roman-occupied territory of Israel? Do you ever feel like that? Like when you are living authentically, as God created you, that you are disappointing and not satisfying others? Perhaps you wish you could bring economic and political satisfaction, but that the word seems to imply something different. Perhaps you wish you could comfort those who are sick with the healing they want, but some other healing seems to be poking its head through. Do you ever feel that the word seems to affirm the depth of who you are and who another is and addresses a deeper need we have than politics or even eternal earthly life can address? Rather, the word asks us to be the very body of Christ in the world, opening our baskets, sitting on hillsides together, refusing the lawmakers' simple equations of who belongs and who doesn't, along with saying even in our illnesses, "you are healed." Do you often feel that the culture is expecting certain things of you that just don't fit what you know God's word calls out of us? It's hard to make these decisions against the many voices in our heads and all around us.

But what if we conceived of God's ways with us, despite the decisions that could cause us trouble? What if we conceived of God's ways with us as a treasure in a field, or a pearl of great value, or like honey in a honeycomb, and more precious than gold? What if we saw joy as the very heartbeat of God's ways with us? What if everything in us refused to compromise that word, that life, that hope, and we clung to the deep sweetness of this word and way, even in the middle of making hard decisions for it?

Sermon Extras

Engaging Kids

Bring a honeycomb in, share it with the kids, and ask them what the psalmist meant when he said that the words of God are sweeter than honeycomb. Ask them: What about the story of Jesus is sweeter than the honeycomb? Can they understand the metaphor? Why didn't Jesus think it was like a sour lemon?

Doing Justice

Take a look at the front page of a newspaper and ask people to look at it from the eyes of God. On what do you base your opinions? Is it on your own self-interest? Is it on what *you* think is good for others? Is it based in the way of the cross?

Seeking Holiness

Have your congregation spend time understanding the sweetness of honey, and the "suffering many things," and what Jesus knew.

Nurturing Creation

The bee who makes the honeycomb is near extinction. Yet, so much of our Old Testament imagery is about the land flowing with milk and honey. Do something to protect bees.

Worship Helps

Opening Prayer

Gracious God, our hearts are restless for you. For you alone, our hearts wait.

[Silence.]

Clear our hearts of anything that would keep us from you as we begin this day, this moment of worship. Keep us clinging to your word, your will, your kingdom. Amen.

Offering Invitation

You are the God of life and love. All of what we have become has been touched and guided by you. May we give out of that abundance. May we give with that knowledge that the only life we want is the one whereby our souls, our spirits, our lifeblood are in sync with the joyful lifeforce that is you. And so, we give you these pennies—pennies that were Caesar's, and we give them to you instead. May they become the power of sweet honey in the honeycomb.

Benediction

Go forth from this place renewed in strength and courage, revived in heart and spirit, and redeemed with the power of a resurrected Christ to live and breathe and be and do what God has in mind for you. Amen and amen.

September 19, 2021– Seventeenth Sunday after Pentecost

Proverbs 31:10-31 or Wisdom of Solomon 1:16–2:1, 12-22 or Jeremiah 11:18-20; Psalm 1 or Psalm 54; James 3:13–4:3, 7-8a; Mark 9:30-37

Jennifer and Todd Pick

Preaching Theme

On any given day, a million things compete for our attention. From one direction comes the tug of the kids' extracurricular activities; from another, the job deadline that is approaching too quickly. There's always yet another bill to be paid, yet another meal to be cooked, yet another news story that proves our inhumanity to one another, yet another...and another....In the midst of all that pulls, tugs, distracts, and preoccupies, how do we open our souls to the breath of the Spirit that leads us back to our main goal of creating beauty, doing justice, and showing kindness?

When we meet Jesus and his disciples in **Mark 9**, Jesus is desperately trying to impart some words of wisdom to his disciples before his impending death. He is reasonably distracted by the future that awaits him in Jerusalem and wants to prepare his disciples as much as possible for the horrific events that will soon take place. Over and again in this Gospel, Jesus tries to warn his disciples of his fate, and each time there rings the familiar refrain, "But [the disciples] didn't understand this kind of talk, and they were afraid to ask him" (Mark 9:32).

I imagine Jesus striding before his baffled disciples with his mind on the future and what God is asking of him, barely registering that there is an argument going on behind him. I also imagine that if the disciples heard Jesus say repeatedly that one day he would be killed, then plans to take up the mantel of leadership might be on their minds. Preoccupied with who among them is the greatest, it's possible they argued about who might best carry on what Jesus had begun. Should it be the strongest among them, the bravest, the wisest, the richest?

In our churches, this scene repeats itself in so many ways. Pastors try to keep the focus on the things of God while those in our congregations argue about everything from the carpet choice to the music selection to the "noise" children make during worship. When the enormity of our task rises before us, we can get overwhelmed and distracted by the minutia of ministry. Perhaps, in these times, it is best to just follow Jesus's example.

Jesus repeats the greatest paradox of the kin-dom of God: "Whoever wants to be first must be least of all and the servant of all" (Mark 9:35). To emphasize his words, he pulls a small child into the conversation and wraps this child up in his arms. There is now a tiny human face directly in front of the Twelve that refocuses their attention. There is nothing like a human face, especially a small one, to reorient priorities—for the disciples and for us. However, Jesus is not done teaching yet. This child's life and how we receive him is a good indication of how we receive the entirety of the kin-dom of God. Even as we read the words of scripture, the meaning of Jesus's words run deeper than what we might realize.

The Greek word for *welcome* used in Mark 9:37, *dexomai*, connotes a literal receiving of someone into one's arms. The picture we should have in our heads is not of someone in an airport quietly holding up a little "Welcome Home" sign on a piece of paper, but of the parent or grandparent down on his or her knees, arms splayed and waiting for their loved one to come running down the ramp into arms opened wide. It is a posture of vulnerability and singular focus on the one who is being welcomed. This Sunday, let's quiet the distractions in our lives long enough to welcome God in every way, especially when God comes in the form of a child who longs to be embraced.

Secondary Preaching Themes

Proverbs and **James** both speak of the humility that is required to live a life with a singular focus on God. Many of us are familiar with Proverbs 31:10-31, which extols the virtues of a good wife or woman. This woman seems to put her family's welfare above her own, ensuring her family's well-being. Recent scholarship has re-defined this woman as Lady Wisdom, who shows up elsewhere in Proverbs. Her qualities, however, must not be stripped entirely from her humanity. She works joyfully with her hands. She reaches out to the needy. She stretches out her hand to the poor. Strength and honor are her clothing. I know this woman, and I'll wager you do as well.

Worship Helps

Gathering Prayer

Holy One, you welcome us into your wide embrace of grace, again and again. As you open your arms to hold our hearts with tender loving-kindness, you invite us to do the same. Open our ears as you call us again to welcome the stranger, the foreigner, the lonely, the outcast, and the weak. Open our hearts to welcome each precious child, just as you have welcomed us. Amen.

Call to Worship

Come, you who are seeking and searching:
there's a community here that's incomplete without you!
In the name of the welcoming One, we gather.
Come, you who are hungry and thirsty:
there's a table here that's incomplete without you!
In the name of the welcoming One, we feast.
Come, you who are weary and worried:
there's a hope here that's incomplete without you!
In the name of the welcoming One, we pray.
Come, you who are lonely and lost:
Christ's body is incomplete without you!
**In the name of the welcoming One, we come
and find that all are welcome here!**

Responsive Reading

Into our lives littered with distraction;
into our bickering, pointless and petty,
**you come among us, welcoming One,
lifting up the littlest and least of us with open arms.**
You come, reminding us to welcome the child.
And by doing so, we welcome God.
You come, reminding us to welcome the stranger.
And by doing so, we welcome angels.
You come, reminding us to welcome the least, the last, and the lost.
And by doing so, we welcome your kin-dom.
When the last are first, and the lowly are lifted;
when the persecuted are blessed, and the weak are strengthened;
when we lose our lives and give them away to love;
**you come among us, welcoming One,
embracing us with open arms.**
When we welcome a child and see the face of God,
**you come among us, welcoming One,
teaching us to be servants of all.**

Benediction

Go out into a weary world, offering the welcome of God.
Go out into places of hostility, offering the hospitality of Christ.
Go out into spaces of brokenness, offering the blessing of the Holy Spirit.
Go and be living, breathing signs of God's realm by offering a wide welcome wherever you go.

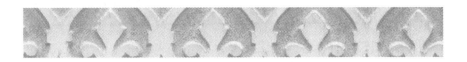

September 26, 2021– Eighteenth Sunday after Pentecost

Esther 7:1-6, 9-10, 9:20-22 or Numbers 11:4-6, 10-16, 24-29; Psalm 124 or Psalm 19:7-14; James 5:13-20; Mark 9:38-50

James F. McIntire

Focusing Prayer

Center me this day, God.
Guide my thoughts, my words, my ideas, my teachings, and my learnings. I receive from you that cup of water that refreshes and renews, and my reward is so great that all I can return is my thanks!
Center, guide, lead, and teach me today and always. Amen.

Preaching Theme

Mark has Jesus offering a peculiar little message about being one-eyed, one-handed, or one-footed. And maybe it has to do with what it brings to your decisions. If you have only one leg, then you are off balance and you have to dive right into the situation before you.

Jesus says that if your hand or your foot causes you to stumble, then you must cut it off because there are just some things in life that you can do better with just one foot or one hand. Not that people with a disability—say, missing a hand or a foot—have that disability because of anyone's sin. But what Jesus does say with this fascinating little metaphor is that to live the life to which God calls us, you sometimes need only one hand, one foot, or one eye—not physically, but metaphorically.

To dive into a situation, maybe it is better to have only one foot. No hesitation. No resistance. You get to the place you wanted to go without a second thought. Jesus's point here is that we need to use that same attitude in living life for God's purposes. No one wants to dive into a situation like that. Most of us prefer to take our time with living our faith, slowly testing the temperature so we can decide if it's really suitable for us before making the commitment.

But Jesus's call is for us to dive in headfirst, no matter the climate, no matter the consequences, no matter the splash you cause—no matter what. You need to make your way to the edge, off balance and wobbly, lean forward and hit the water of faith like never before. There are places where we would not go if we had that chance to walk away but Jesus wants us at the edge of a place where having only one hand or one foot is better than two, a place where maybe we're feeling off-balance, a place where God asks us to confidently commit to the headfirst dive that God requires of each of us.

We need each other. That's the very foundation of our faith as followers of Jesus. Never was our faith meant to be lived out separately in a vacuum. "For where two or three are gathered in my name," says Jesus, "I'm there with them" (**Matt 18:20**). Faith lived out is a public venture, not private. I need you as much as you need me—I might have two hands and two feet and two eyes, but what I need of you requires that we each give up a hand, a foot, an eye, and give up that balance that keeps us so comfortable. What we need each other for requires that we dive into each other's lives, into the sacred places of our world, into the moments when we have doubt, into the spaces where justice is absent, into the lives around us struggling for existence.

Stand on one foot, says Jesus, slightly off balance, lean forward, dive in. It's what we need of each other.

Sermon Extras

Seeking Holiness

"Salt is good; but if salt loses its saltiness, how will it become salty again? Maintain salt among yourselves and keep peace with each other" (**Mark 9:50a-b**).

We take salt for granted—mostly granulated, iodized salt for us—the saltshaker on the table, salted butter, salted pork, salted popcorn, but also the salt water that we swim in or salt that has a medicinal use, or salt used to melt the snow. Whenever we want it, we have access to salt, but for most of history salt was one of the most precious of commodities.

Salt was included by the ancient Egyptians as an offering in tombs at the funerals of respected people and was one of the key elements in the development of civilization around the world. Salt was used by conquering armies who would spread it on conquered cities to symbolize a curse on its rehabilitation—"salting the earth."

Salt became so valuable because it was highly desired as a seasoning, for curing foods, or for healing properties. Also, it was valuable because it was so difficult to obtain. Salt was first developed for people's use simply by evaporating the water from saltwater or by collecting it from the edges of seas. Later, as mining for salt became more common, salt roads developed throughout Europe, North Africa, and Asia—trade routes for getting salt from the mines to the markets where it could be sold.

It's been said that Roman soldiers were sometimes paid with salt and that eventually the word *salary* came from money that Roman soldiers were given so they could buy salt. The Roman Empire controlled the price of salt, increasing its price to raise money for wars, or lowering its price to ensure that the poorest citizens could easily afford this important part of their diet. Caravans consisting of as many as forty thousand camels traversed four hundred miles of the Sahara bearing salt to inland markets, and sometimes trading salt for slaves. For example, Timbuktu was a huge salt and slave market.

What does Jesus mean when he says, "You are the salt of the earth" (**Matt 5:13**)? Are we as precious and valuable as salt? And what does Jesus mean when he says, "If salt loses its saltiness, how will it become salty again?" (Mark 9:50)? Can salt without its saltiness ever become salty again?

Worship Helps

Call to Worship (Based on Psalm 19:7-14)

God's instruction is perfect, reviving one's very being.
> Revive us, O God!

God's laws are faithful, making naive people wise.
> Guide us, O God!

God's regulations are right, gladdening the heart.
> Give light to our lives, O God!

God's judgments are true.
> More desirable than tons of pure gold! Sweeter than honey dripping off the honeycomb!

We are enlightened by what God teaches,
> Clear me, God, of any unknown sin and save us from willful sins.

Let the words of my mouth and the meditations of my heart be pleasing to you, O God,
> my rock and my redeemer.

October 3, 2021–Nineteenth Sunday after Pentecost

Job 1:1, 2:1-10 or Genesis 2:18-24; Psalm 26 or Psalm 8; Hebrews 1:1-4, 2:5-12; Mark 10:2-16

Kirsten S. Oh

Preaching Theme

As a mother of a toddler, I am afforded the otherwise forgotten opportunity to watch children's programing on television. One of such delights is a TV program that is derived from *Mister Rogers' Neighborhood* in which Daniel Tiger and his family live in the Neighborhood of Make-Believe. In this program children are taught wonderful lessons from waiting patiently for a duck to hatch to allowing anger to be shown but not hurting someone because of it, through cute and catchy jingles. This musical lesson is repeated throughout the thirty-minute program with the purpose that children learn it and then hum or sing it throughout the day. One of these programs was about enjoying the present moment and not allowing it to pass by because you are caught in your own futuristic wants (like being sad about a lost toy during bubble bath time) or distractions from too many choices (like so many good books at the library). The jingle for that program was "Enjoy the 'WOW' that's happening now."[1] My daughter and I must have sung that jingle thirty-some times or more after watching the show in the late afternoon. And I still sing it often to my toddler when past complaints, present distractions, or future worries or wants take over the enjoyment that is present in the moment.

In **Mark 10:13-16**, Jesus is faced with his disciples preventing earnest parents from bringing their children to him. In our text, readers may assume that the disciples considered these children distractions from more important tasks with more important people. While the disciples may have thought they were doing their job, Jesus scolds his disciples with indignation or ἠγανάκτησεν. In Greek, indignation is a strong, emotional word that denotes anger at perceived injustice. Jesus explains his indignation—"You may not know this, but to them, the ones you are currently forbidding, belong the kingdom of God" (Mark 10:14, paraphrased). The same word is used by the disciples themselves when James and John request the prime seat in Jesus's new kingdom (**Mark 10:41**) and when the woman anoints Jesus with expensive perfume (**Mark 14:4**).

This is the only time Jesus expresses this emotion in Mark and his indignation comes after an earlier teaching when Jesus found the disciples arguing about who among them were the greatest: "He sat down, called the twelve, and said to them, 'Whoever wants to be first must be last of all and servant of all.' Then he took a little child and put it among them; and taking it in his arms, he said to them, 'Whoever welcomes one such child in my name welcomes me'" (**Mark 9:35-37** NRSV).

Children were conferred a lower status within the traditional Jewish custom as well as Greco-Roman culture, as can be seen by their inability to participate in religious practices. Similarly, their lower status may have limited their chances to receive such blessings to infrequent and strict circumstances. However, the moment was upon them, and parents had brought their children for this holy man to bestow a blessing on them. Enjoy the wow that's happening now. These children are the very examples of the ones who will inherit the kingdom of God: "They therefore have every right to approach Jesus and be blessed by him."[2] Jesus captures the moment and invites this interaction.

Unlike the disciples, we find Jesus practicing what the Jesuits and the Fransiscans call the "Sacrament of the Present moment." According to Franciscan author, Terry Hershey, "Jean-Pierre de Caussade (ordained member of the Society of Jesus) wrote about the sacrament of the present moment. We are invited to choose to live each day as a sacrament (as a gift), enabling us to see, to hear, to taste, and to touch grace—the goodness of God's presence in our world."[3] It did not matter to Jesus that children were of a lower status or that blessings were generally restricted to prescribed times and places. He saw what the present moment was offering and lived up to the sacrament of receiving this gift of interaction with the children.

Considering Jesus's invitation to the children to fully participate in worship, Eugene Boring writes, "Jesus thus is saying that 'status and attainment' are not prerequisites of the Kingdom; rather it is based upon God's grace."[4] Jesus's subversive act opens up the answer to the question, "Who then can enter the Kingdom of God?" With rebuke in his tone, Jesus says to his disciples, "Allow the children to come to me. Don't forbid them, because God's kingdom belongs to people like these children. I assure you that whoever doesn't welcome God's kingdom like a child will never enter it" (Mark 10:14-15).

In many ways, Mark 10 draws us to Jesus's responsiveness and receptivity to children. He takes time to enjoy the wow of the children who were coming to him rather than being distracted by other perhaps "weightier" matters or persons to attend to. This passage asks the question, "Who in our society are considered of lower, different, or foreign status and what is the sacrament of relating with these people who are created equally in the image of God?" Mark's Gospel chronicles the active ministry of Jesus with a clarion call to the disciples that they too need to "take up their cross" and follow him (**Mark 8:34**). This injunction is embedded in the teachings of Mark 10 regarding discipleship and God's kingdom. If we are to be followers of Christ in 2021, what should we learn from the sacrament of the present moment and how are we to welcome the gift of all persons?

Sermon Extras

Seeking Holiness

After the sermon or at a later time of guided reflection, give each person a sheet of paper with the questions asked in the previous section.

1. Who in our society are considered of lower, different, or foreign status? What is the sacrament of relating with these persons who are created equally in the image of God?

2. What do we learn from the sacrament of the present moment and how are we to welcome the gift of all persons?

3. What does the sacrament of the present moment mean and what would welcoming the gift of all people look like to you?

As each member of the congregation answers these questions reflectively, see if there is a particular group of people who resonate with some consensus from the congregation. Consider a congregation-wide activity to invite, engage, interact, and minister with these persons in ongoing, meaningful ways.

Worship Helps

Gathering Prayer

Creator God,
You welcome and love all those whom you have created and are made in your image.
Help us to see the mystery of your image in all beings small and big and
teach us to enjoy the beauty of one another in ordinary, everyday moments.
Amen.

Call to Worship (Based on Psalm 8 and Hebrews 2:6-8)

O Lord, our Lord, how majestic is your name in all the earth!
When I look at your heavens, the work of your fingers, the moon and the stars, which you have set in place,
What is man, that you are mindful of him, or the son of man, that you care for him?
You made him for a little while lower than the angels, you have crowned him with glory and honor.
ALL: O Lord, our Lord, how majestic is your name in all the earth!

Benediction

May the creator God,
whose name is majestic in all the earth, bless you by enabling you to see, to hear, to taste,
and to touch grace—the goodness of God's presence in our world.

May the one who set the heavens, the moon and the stars, also set your hearts in order
that you may exhibit the responsiveness and receptivity of Jesus toward all persons in the
sacredness of your everyday lives.
Amen.

October 10, 2021–Twentieth Sunday after Pentecost

Job 23:1-9, 16-17 or Amos 5:6-7, 10-15; Psalm 22:1-15 or Psalm 90:12-17; Hebrews 4:12-16; Mark 10:17-31

Ernest S. Lyght

Preaching Theme

Our text (**Job 23:1-9, 16-17**) should be framed with the beginning and ending verses of the book of Job. First, **1:1** describes Job: "That man was honest, a person of absolute integrity; he feared God and avoided evil." Job and his wife had seven sons and three daughters. Job was very wealthy, owning thousands of sheep, camels, oxen, and donkeys. He also had a huge number of servants. Job could be described as a pious man who was living a happy life. However, this life of bliss came to an abrupt end when Job's material possessions were destroyed and his children were killed in a natural disaster. The Adversary was wreaking havoc in Job's life. Second, Job's story ends with an epilogue (**42:7-17**). After all that Job endured, "the LORD blessed Job's latter days more than his former ones" (42:12a). His wealth was restored, he was blessed with more children, and Job died "old and satisfied" (42:17). It is in the context of these bookends and the continuing season of Pentecost that we want to examine our text. The dominant theme is our understanding of the presence of God, the nearness of God, and God's hiddenness. Job has suffered much and he seems to have no resolution to his situation. He wants some resolve and relief. Job wants to plead his case before God again, so he comes prepared with his oral arguments. He no longer can accept or tolerate his suffering and pain; therefore, he wants to challenge God. Job wants to enter into God's presence. Note here that God does not play hide-and-seek.

The theme of God's presence also intersects with another theme that manifests itself in the form of a question: Why do the righteous suffer? We live in an imperfect world. Jesus Christ, however, brings us hope in the midst of the good and the bad. Theologians tackle Job's plight as a matter of theodicy. Theodicy, of course, is an effort to give meaning to the idea of a perfect God who allows pain to exist among people. Job wants an answer to his questions regarding his own suffering. Is not God nearby? Is God concerned about what has happened to him? Does God care about him? Unknown to Job, God had placed some limitations on what could be done to

Job: "The LORD said to the Adversary, 'Look, all he has is within your power; only don't stretch out your hand against him'" (**Job 1:12**). God cared deeply about Job, but Job did not know it at the time. Job did believe that God would listen to him if he could be found. He laments that he is not able to find God. He wants to find God and "grasp" God. The point is that God is apparently absent. Yet, we know that God is never absent, because God is always near, present even in God's hiddenness. Jesus, too, wondered whether God had left him all alone (**Ps 22:1**). First, God chooses the venue, and the circumstances of God's presence. Second, we have a standing invitation to come into God's presence. Jesus said, "Come to me, all you who are struggling hard and carrying heavy loads, and I will give you rest" (**Matt 11:28**). Third, in the midst of life's storms, we are never alone. In his despair, Job has found neither human nor divine comfort. Job is persistent, even though he has found no relief by the end of chapter 23. In this whole process, Job displays the character of a person who has a deep relationship with God. His wife suggested that he should "curse God and die" (**Job 2:9**). In his response to her, Job acknowledged that we will receive good and bad from God. Job is able to ask the tough questions because of his relationship with God. Could not God have given Job an answer to his question, "Why me?" But God has a time line, and God is always on time.

Sermon Extras

Seeking Holiness

The theme that winds its way from **Job 23** through the other three texts (**Amos 5**, **Hebrews 4**, and **Mark 10**) is the need for a growing relationship with God. We need to reach out to the Lord: "Seek the LORD and live" (Amos 5:6). Amos encourages the people to "seek good and not evil, that you may live" (Amos 5:14). The Hebrews text reminds us that no one can hide from God. Consider this invitation: "Finally, let's draw near to the throne of favor with confidence so that we can receive mercy and find grace when we need help" (Heb 4:16). The Mark text is also an invitation to "draw near to the throne of grace." Jesus told the rich man to sell what he owned and follow him. When we follow Jesus, we are able to enter into a new relationship with God. There is no pecking order when we follow Jesus because the first will be last and the last will be first.

An intriguing theme that can be illustrated is the tension between justice and mercy. A story was told about a speeding motorist who was stopped by a police officer. Justice would call for the person to receive a traffic ticket. Mercy would allow for the issuance of a warning. Which alternative is most desirable, and on what grounds?

Worship Helps

Call to Worship

We gather together to worship God in spirit and in truth. Allow the quietness of God's presence to bring calm to our wandering minds and troubled souls. We have come to worship God.

Benediction

We have worshipped in God's presence. Go out into the community and serve in God's presence.

October 17, 2021–Twenty-First Sunday after Pentecost

Job 38:1-7 (34-41) or Isaiah 53:4-12; Psalm 104:1-9, 24, 35b or Psalm 91:9-16; Hebrews 5:1-10; Mark 10:35-45

Grace S. Pak

Preaching Theme

James and John, the sons of Zebedee, came to Jesus asking for seats on his right and his left when Jesus comes into power, and to be made leaders with a lot of control and influence. When they heard about this, other disciples "became angry with James and John" (**Mark 10:41**), perhaps because they also wanted these positions of power and these two brothers beat them to it. This story tells us two things that haven't changed in the last two thousand years: (1) humans' innate desire to be leaders and to be in positions of power, and (2) our understanding and the practice of leadership.

It seems it is a part of human nature to crave power and control. Just like James, John, and Jesus's disciples, it is not uncommon to see people vie for positions of power in any organization, whether it's in church, work, or in politics. There is something about being in the power seat and having control that is very attractive. Some are very active, like James and John, in seeking the power seat. Others are subtle and passive, like the disciples, and are resentful when others usurp the power seat. This story shows how the struggle for power keeps us hostage and blinds us to the realities of God's kin-dom, which calls on us to love others as Jesus loved us.

According to the Learner's Dictionary, the definition of *leader* is "a powerful person who controls or influences what other people do: a person who leads a group, organization, country, etc."[5] Businessdictionary.com defines *leader* as "a person or thing that holds a dominant or superior position within its field, and is able to exercise a high degree of control or influence over others."[6]

Jesus defined the leadership of his day when he said, "You know that the ones who are considered the rulers by the Gentiles show off their authority over them and their high-ranking officials order them around" (Mark 10:42). Clearly, the understanding and practice of leadership has not changed much over the last two thousand years.

Jesus uses this incident and the grumbling among his disciples as a teaching moment to redefine leadership. Antithetical to the conventional definition and practice of leadership, Jesus says, "Whoever wants to be great among you will be your servant. Whoever wants to be first among you will be the slave of all" (vv. 43-44). For Jesus, a leader is not someone who exercises power over others but one who is willing to forego one's needs and desires for the sake of others.

One illustration of a leader akin to Jesus's teaching is geese flying in a "V" formation. The lead goose takes the brunt of all the drag and resistance of the air so that other geese have an easier time flying behind. The leader is the one who is willing to do the hard work so that the others are helped.

Jesus identifies himself as the leader who "didn't come to be served but rather to serve and to give his life to liberate many people" (v. 45). Jesus, in his example, shows the inversion of what great means. Greatness is not about how many people you lord over, but how many you serve and love. To say that we are followers of Jesus Christ means to do what he exemplified in his life. Everybody is in a position of power over somebody. Parents are in a position of power over children, teachers over students, pastors over laity, laity over pastors, strong over weak, employer over employee, dominant group over nondominant, and so on. But anybody can be a *great* leader by choosing Jesus's leadership.

In imitating Jesus's leadership, we are liberated from our own desires and need for self-validation by seeking to serve others rather than to exercise our power and privilege over others.

As disciples of Jesus Christ, who are the ones God put around you to serve?

What are specific ways you can be a great leader for them?

How are we, the church, serving the communities around us?

What does it look like for the church to "be the slave of all"?

Sermon Extras

Engaging Kids

Ask the children, "Who do you think is a leader?" Have a large and heavy object nearby.

In front of the children, have one person lift the object with ease and another person struggle to lift it. Ask the children again, "Who do you think is a leader? One who is strong or one who is weak?" Give the children a moment to respond. Then say, "Jesus said, 'Whoever wants to be great among you will be your servant. Whoever wants to be first among you will be the slave of all'" (**Mark 10:43-44**). Then ask, "What is Jesus saying?" Ask for responses. Then say, "What Jesus is saying is that it is not the strong person who is a leader, but the one who helps others is the leader. That is what Jesus showed us through everything he did. Jesus gave his life to help us have a better life."

Worship Helps

Call to Worship

Come, let us worship God, who is enthroned above and yet who loves us!
We worship you, O God.
Come, let us follow Jesus Christ, our example for loving God and others!
We follow you, Jesus Christ.
Come, let us open our hearts to the Holy Spirit, who gives us strength and courage to be servants to all!
We open our hearts to you, Holy Spirit. Amen.

Prayer of Repentance

Lord Jesus, you have come to our world not to be served but rather to serve and to give your life to save us. Because you love us, you willingly gave up your power and privilege and took on human form to walk among us, to laugh with us, to cry with us, and to suffer for us. We confess and repent that we do not want to give up our power and privilege. We strive to amass as much power and privilege as we can to power over others rather than use them to serve others. Holy Spirit, help us and give us courage to follow Jesus's example so that in our serving, the world will be changed and reflect your kin-dom. In your name we pray. Amen.

Sending Forth

We live in a world where people vie for positions of power and the powerful oppressing the powerless is the norm. As followers of Jesus Christ, we march to a different beat. We are called to be leaders who serve and benefit others. May you be the leader at home, at work, at school, in your neighborhood, and wherever you may be throughout the week by serving others and that through you God may be glorified and God's kin-dom built up! Amen.

October 24, 2021–Twenty-Second Sunday after Pentecost

Job 42:1-6, 10-17 or Jeremiah 31:7-9; Psalm 34:1-8 (19-22) or Psalm 126; Hebrews 7:23-28; Mark 10:46-52

Sheila M. Beckford

Preaching Theme

Religious institutions are known to hire consultants and experts to pinpoint the reason for the decline in church membership. Cumulative results point to outdated theology, lukewarm theology, liberal theology versus conservative theology, and many other factors by which people leave the church. After reading and hearing stories and testimonies from some people who have exited the church, it seems that a genie-in-a-bottle theology is linked to each. You know, the theology that makes God into this magical being on whom one can call to make everything in their life right, or the thought that those who believe will not suffer or experience any complications or conflicts? We call this bad theology. The cliché "God is always right on time" did not manifest in their lives when they suffered through sexual assault, abandonment, being wrongfully convicted and incarcerated, or during the death of a child (whether natural or accidental). The complaint was that although they were faithful, God still allowed them to experience suffering. How could those of us who were faithful suffer so much? "Did God not care that we are drowning" is the sentiment of each broken heart (**Mark 4:37**, paraphrased).

For me, the book of **Job** is one of the most challenging and troubling. Not because I ascribe to the genie-in-a-bottle theology, but because I cannot imagine the pain of losing a child, much less children and forgetting about the pain once more children were born. As preachers, we tend to gloss over this problematic text to jump straight to the divine restoration of Job's status and wealth. We cannot overlook Job and his wife's continued pain and suffering, and the physical, spiritual, and emotional scars that existed after losing their children. We cannot ignore Job's struggle with his faith through their trauma and loss. How does one resolve this scripture, which suggests that God not only let this suffering happen but also instigated it?

We cannot justify the suffering with God's restoration or blessing of "double the portion." Job 42:1-6, 10-17 requires us, the reader, to go deeper, not just into the book of Job, but also into our lives.

I hope that we do not take the "defending God approach." In doing so, we say the words I have heard preached many times: "Job got it all back." However, if we look at this text through the lens of suffering, this scripture is not about exonerating God but is a message to us all that God has "no partiality to humans" (**Job 32:21**, paraphrased). Suffering is a human condition that we will all experience. There will be moments where we cannot understand why we are going through pains and anguish at the hands of those we trust. We will suffer the pain of death, physical illness, and even spiritual weakness and remind ourselves and the Lord just how good we've been.

Suffering has no partiality. It transcends culture, faithfulness, belief, or unbelief. The book of Job reminds us that when we suffer, we get closer to God. It is an opportunity to hear God, to build a relationship with God, and to trust God. Job admitted that he only knew of God but did not know God. It was through his struggles that he reached out and knew God as his God.

The genie-in-a-bottle theology causes people to suffer needlessly. It compounds the physical and emotional pain by adding a spiritual dynamic.

Sermon Extras

Seeking Holiness

People respond differently to suffering. Some isolate themselves from others and even try to separate themselves from God. Some complain because it hurts to suffer. Some give up and fall into a deep depression. Regardless of how one handles the stages of suffering, we must honor their story. The book of **Job** gives us ideas to assist those who are suffering: (1) listen, (2) empathize, (3) pray for them, (4) ask to pray with them, (5) show up without judgment, (6) avoid blaming the person who is suffering for their own pain, and (7) believe that God is walking with us through the journey.

Worship Helps

Call to Worship

We bless your name, O Lord.
Through the weary days and the weary nights,
we bless your name O, Lord.
While walking through the shadows of illness and death,

we bless your name, O Lord.
When filled with questions and demanding answers,
we bless your name, O Lord.
While seeking relief from our pains,
we bless your name, O Lord.
We remember you, God, even in times of questioning, suffering, and waiting. For it is you who walks with us during the times of trials. It is you who will come to our defense and it is you who will deliver us from our times of sorrow. Amen.

Centering Prayer

As we continue to breathe in the transformative power of Pentecost, we will take this time to breathe! Breathe in the aroma of God's peace. Breathe out the stress from the week, breathe in the love of God. Breathe out the challenges and obstacles. Now, let God know your struggles.

[Silence.]

Amen.

Sending Forth

Lord, we have come into this place of worship seeking answers to our questions: Why? Why me? Why now? Why am I suffering? We are leaving with the response that it is the human condition to suffer, but that God the divine walks with us, suffers with us, and helps us through the journey. God, let your presence be known and felt. Do not hide yourself from us and remove our blindness to see you in the midst of our trials. Send us your peace. Amen.

October 31, 2021–Twenty-Third Sunday after Pentecost

Ruth 1:1-18 or Deuteronomy 6:1-9; Psalm 146 or Psalm 119:1-8; Hebrews 9:11-14; Mark 12:28-34

Meredith E. Hoxie Schol

Preaching Theme

On All Saints Sunday, the church remembers and prays for the communion of saints who have died in the previous year. In my local church, we frequently invite people to bring a picture or an object that reminds us of these people, and we set up a space in the sanctuary where these items are displayed and prayed over. Seeing these pictures assembled, running our hands along the crocheted blankets, smelling a favorite flower from a loved one's garden; the tangible, tactile encounter with these little altars provides a powerful tool for remembering.

In the **Deuteronomy** passage, we read the Shema: "Hear, O Israel: The Lord is our God, the Lord alone. You shall love the Lord your God with all your heart, and with all your soul, and with all your might" (Deut 6:4-5 NRSV).

This command is at the heart of God's covenant with Israel. The children of God are then given clear instructions on how to help with the remembering:

> Keep these words that I am commanding you today in your heart. Recite them to your children and talk about them when you are at home and when you are away, when you lie down and when you rise. Bind them as a sign on your hand, fix them as an emblem on your forehead, and write them on the doorposts of your house and on your gates. (Deut 6:6-9 NRSV)

These outward signs and symbols were constant reminders of this central commandment to love God throughout the day. They helped the people to ritualize even the simplest activities, walking in or out of their homes, engaging in conversations with their children, and so on. With this command constantly before them, it was easy to call it to mind when they needed a reminder of the covenantal love they shared with God.

All Saints Sunday provides a special opportunity for us to reflect on the ways our ordinary practices and places call us to remember. As we tell stories and hold photos, or sit in the old rocking chair we once shared with a parent or child, we are tied to the memories of those who came before us.

A sermon on this passage could turn to psychology or educational theory to highlight connections between physical objects and memory, but for familiarity's sake, one could also consider the many church rituals and practices centered around similar physical objects and symbols. The elements we taste, touch, and share tie us to the practices of the saints throughout the life of the church. Invite the hearers of this word to consider what objects or spaces might help to provide daily reminders of their connection to their loved ones, to their church community, and to the Lord our God.

Sermon Extras

Engaging Kids

Materials: Ribbon or yarn.

Lesson: Talk about the tradition of tying a ribbon around your finger at the moment you memorize something that you don't want to forget.

You can say something, such as: Our brains are really complicated, and they process information constantly. Tying a ribbon around our finger is a way of associating a physical action with a particular thought or memory so that we give our brain multiple inputs about one thing, which may help your brain retrieve that information later.

Seeking Holiness

Materials: An object that reminds you of a loved one who has died, such as a picture, something they made, flowers, or baked goods they liked.

Focusing act: Spend time holding this object. Let the memories that tie this object to your loved one come into your consciousness. Give yourself the space to feel the range of emotions that may emerge for you.

Prayer: As you turn to God in prayer, give thanks for the life of your loved one. Name the ways they shaped and formed your own life of faith.

Worship Helps

Gathering Prayer

God to whom the saints have prayed,
As we gather to worship on this All Saints Sunday, we are particularly mindful of the life, ministry, and witness of those who have died this year. These are the friends and family,

parents, siblings, and children with whom our earthly journeying has ended, but whose memory we carry with us and call upon when we remember our great cloud of witnesses. As we remember them and as we have come to know them through their time with us, may we also remember the promise of resurrection, which we know through the witness of your son, Jesus.
Amen.

Call to Worship

Hear this, family of God: the Lord our God, the Lord is one.
Let us worship the Lord our God, just as the saint before us, with all our hearts, and with all our souls, and with all our minds, and with all our strength.

Hear this, family of God: the Lord our God, the Lord is one.
Let us worship the Lord our God and teach our children who come after us, as we love our neighbor as ourselves.

There are no commandments greater than these.
We will remember them, and we will remember those who taught them to us.
We will remember them, and we will teach them to our children.

Benediction

Remember:
each time you pick up a piece of bread,
each time water splashes your hand,
each time you raise a cup to your lips.

Remember:
the saints who have gone before you,
the children who look to you,
the Lord our God who has been, and will be, with us through it all.

November 7, 2021– All Saints Sunday

Ruth 3:1-5, 4:13-17 or 1 Kings 17:8-16; Psalm 127 or Psalm 146; Hebrews 9:24-28; Mark 12:38-44

Ernest S. Lyght

Preaching Theme

Elijah, the main subject of our text (**1 Kgs 17**), was a Hebrew prophet and miracle-worker who boldly stood for God, just as we are called to stand confidently for Jesus today. Living in a time of idolatry, the name Elijah meant "My God is Yahweh." Elijah was active during the reign of King Ahab and Queen Jezebel in the ninth century BC. He confronted the royal couple over their idolatry of the Canaanite god, Ba'al. In dramatic fashion, at the end of his life, he was carried to heaven in a chariot of fire. Elijah displayed an abiding faith in God and an incredible trust in God. He went before King Ahab and announced God's curse: "As surely as the LORD lives, Israel's God, the one I serve, there will be neither dew nor rain these years unless I say so" (**1 Kgs 17:1**). It was then that the Lord directed Elijah to flee and hide by the Cherith Brook east of the Jordan River. While there, he had water to drink as well as the bread and meat that the ravens had brought to him. His basic needs were being cared for by God. Such comforts could entice a person to hang around for a long time, but that result was not in the Lord's game plan.

Our text has a focus on God's plan. Elijah realized a change in God's plan when the brook dried up from a lack of rain in the land. Remember God's promise in verse 1? What dry spots have you encountered in your life, and what was your reaction? Perhaps Elijah wanted to stay on, but instead, he followed God's directions. God sent him to live with a widow in Zarephath. This act is yet another demonstration of obedience that is woven into the fabric of this text. Elijah was an eyewitness to God's miraculous activity. After arriving at the widow's home, Elijah blessed the woman's scant supply of oil and flour. The resulting miracle provided enough oil and flour to last for many days. In this scene we also witness the woman's obedience. She willingly followed Elijah's directions. She shared her minuscule resources with a stranger. Would we be willing to follow such directions? How will we treat strangers who knock on the church door when it is midnight in their lives?

At the time, there had been an economic collapse in the nation due to a severe drought, which ruined crops and brought death among the people. It is God who sent the drought, but God was active in the present and future of the nation. The text, therefore, has to be interpreted in the context of the whole book of Kings in general, and the seventeenth chapter in particular. God feeds the prophet who has the task of confronting the religious and political tensions. King Ahab's religious policies trigger the drought. There was a contest between the prophets of competing religions, which exacerbated the duration of the drought because the people did not immediately do God's will. The contest is resolved when clouds appear on the horizon (**1 Kgs 18:44-45**). As a pastor, preacher, or prophet, are you willing to confront the principalities and powers in our society or in your community? How will you do this? In this story, God speaks. God is at the center of the story, and it is a matter of our obedience to God. Why was Elijah obedient to God? Why was the widow obedient to Elijah's request and directions? Why should contemporary Christians be obedient to God? In what ways are we disobedient to God? God sent Elijah who, in fact, saves the widow from near starvation and death. In saving her, we see a demonstration of how God cares for the people of the world. God, however, expects obedience and faithfulness. God, who has the last word, does not ignore the victims of poverty and government mismanagement at the hands of kings, queens, and presidents.

Sermon Extras

Engaging Kids

There are several common themes that thread their way through the additional lectionary texts: obedience, trust, giving thanks, and following directions. In the **Ruth** text, Naomi seeks security for Ruth. Ruth follows Naomi's instructions, demonstrating her obedience. The **Hebrew** texts reminds us that we belong to God, who sent Jesus into the world. Jesus obeys his Father, sacrificing his life for our sins. The **Mark** text also reveals the principle of sacrifice. The poor widow sacrificed her limited funds. In her poverty, she was obedient to her religious beliefs and sacrificed the widow's mite. A clear lesson is that Christ's disciples should never do anything that robs God because we cannot beat God's generous giving to us. **Psalm 127** affirms the belief that we are in the hands of God, who created us. **Psalm 146** invites us to trust the Lord, realizing that God is our helper because God cares about us. We, therefore, should praise the Lord at all times.

A children's sermon can be developed based on one of these several themes: obedience, trust, giving thanks, following directions, and sharing.

Worship Helps

Gathering Prayer

Caring God, help us always to be mindful of your abundant love in our preaching, teaching, serving, and reaching out to the poor and folks who are in desperate need.

Offertory Prayer

We thank you, Lord, for the showers of blessings in our lives. Help us to assume an attitude of gratitude in our giving, knowing that your gifts will oversupply our needs. Today, we cherish the opportunity to share our gifts.

Benediction

Go forth into the world and look for opportunities to share your many gifts in the work of God's kingdom-building. Go out into your community and stand up for justice, in the name of Jesus.

November 14, 2021– Twenty-Fifth Sunday after Pentecost

1 Samuel 1:4-20 or Daniel 12:1-3; 1 Samuel 2:1-10 or Psalm 16; Hebrews 10:11-14 (15-18), 19-25; Mark 13:1-8

Lydia Muñoz

Preaching Theme

Holiness is a term that has been thrown around these days, it seems, for convenience's sake. It seems especially appropriate when we want to bolster our point of view or our opinion, particularly when it comes to issues of morality. It is as if holiness rests solely on us when the writer of Hebrews reminds us that holiness is now written in our hearts by the one who, through love, sees us as we truly are: good and of sacred worth. Our holiness is based on God's love for us, as demonstrated through Jesus Christ, who opens this reality to everyone who believes that this covenant was made for, and with, them.

Our holiness has nothing to do with our ability to act holy. When I was a volleyball player in high school and college, I remember how our coach trained us to rise to the level of play that she saw in us from the beginning. She knew that the level of your game rises as you begin to internalize positive messages and to understand how good plays come together and what is expected of you and your role in the team. Your level of play can also rise up when you practice and play with players that may be at a higher level of play than you and can give you support and encouragement. Holiness is one of those things that is both here and not yet here; it's not yet here because we have a hard time perceiving that we, too, are holy. It is here because God makes it possible through Jesus, the firstborn, the great high priest. This is the ultimate miracle of incarnation, the ability to connect with us in such a way that we now look like Christ and Christ like us, like a couple who can finish each other's sentences in that special intimate way.

I get it. When the cares of life are pulling at you and you're bogged down by deadlines and traffic, when your homelife is a mess, it's hard to even conceive that the writer of **Hebrews** has us in mind. It's probably because we have been bombarded by the great examples of holiness that are held up as the preferred option. You know them: people like Gandhi, Mother Teresa, and Father Richard Rohr (just to name a few of the ones who have influenced my life). However, sometimes I feel that this kind of holiness is just a setup for failure. I can never be Gandhi or Mother Teresa; I wouldn't even have a clue how to start. When I was a kid, a favorite movie of mine to watch at Christmastime was *The Bells of Saint Mary's* with Ingrid Bergman. For me, she was the epitome of what holiness was supposed to look like. She was sublime, beautiful, patient, and loving; yet she had a feisty side to her that played sports and taught boxing. I wanted to be just like her. The truth is that none of them, not even Ingrid, worked. But that's just the point, isn't it?

God loves us so much that God became one of us, just like us. God comes to us, as one of us. Our holiness is found in our ability to discover this incarnational God who steps into our reality, into our beautiful mess, and that's what makes it holy.

Holiness just might mean that we make it through our morning devotions for a full hour and somedays we barely remember to say "thank you, God" just before our head hits the pillow at night. Maybe holiness is about remembering that at any moment, when our hearts are inclined, the Holy of Holies is open to us anytime and anywhere. Perhaps it's that moment when we notice the changing leaves and the changing seasons around us from fall to winter. Perhaps it's the moment when we see our child's smile at the anticipation that Christmas season will soon be here. It's definitely in the moment when we are together that holiness is most notable. Our greatest reminder that we are holy is each other. We can never be more holy than when we are in each other's presence. Together, we are the body of Christ, the ones "he has made perfect forever those who are being made holy" to do good work together (Heb 10:14 NIV). So, we need to remind and encourage each other with these words of hope, not as a weapon of judgment to hold against each other, but as peace written in our hearts and sealed by love itself. And this will never pass away, even if heaven and earth do.

Sermon Extras

Seeking Holiness

Holiness is a hard term to engage people in and with, and most of the time it has to do with the term not being accessible for most of us. Many of us do not think that we, too, can be considered among the holy, or think that others are considered holy as well. Try this spiritual exercise for homework this week: invite your congregation or your small groups to practice seeing holiness in ordinary places, like at the supermarket, a gas station, or the local convenience store. The task is to notice the people and, instead of looking away, to look at their faces and pray to yourself: "The Holy One in me greets the Holy One in you." Or, to pray: "The Divine in me sees the Divine in you." After a week of doing this, ask people what happened. It's a great way to start a time of sharing within the worship experience that moves people from being just *hearers* to being *doers* of the word, and it's a great conversation starter.

Worship Helps

Gathering Prayer

God of all who cry out to you, help us know and believe that even when you are silent, you are still listening. Amen.

Call to Worship (Based on Psalm 16)

Let all those who trust in the Lord gather together in freedom.
In you, O God, we put our trust, and our hearts celebrate in your joy!
God makes a home for all those who are seeking to rest in safety.
You, O God, will never let those who faithfully follow you fall into a pit.
Therefore, let us rejoice in the One who calls us beautiful!
You teach us the way of life and, in you, our hearts can breathe in peace.

[Consider a sung response here, such as: "Open My Heart" by Ana Hernandez.]

Prayers of the People (Based on 1 Samuel 1:4-20)

[Allow people to respond to each section, either aloud or in their hearts.]

God, just like you heard Hannah's cry, you turn your ears toward our prayers as we come to you for…
The poor, the widow, and the orphan who suffer at the hands of the powerful…
Those who suffer the pain and violence of war…
   Lord in your mercy, **hear our cry.**
Those who suffer in silence with the pain of depression and mental anguish…
   Lord in your mercy, **hear our cry.**
Those who are ravaged by addiction…
   Lord in your mercy, **hear our cry.**
Those who are separated from their children at the border, and for all children looking for a home…
   Lord in your mercy, **hear our cry.**
Those whose children have become trapped in the industrial prison complex…
   Lord in your mercy, **hear our cry.**
Those whose ears and hearts are closed to the cries of the world…
   Lord in your mercy, **change our hearts.**

Sending Forth (Based on Hebrews 10)

Beloved! You, yes, even you have been called holy by a holy God!
   In the midst of trials and troubles…
   We are holy because God said so.
   When we are at our worst…

We are holy because God said so.
When those around us can't see our sacred value...
We are holy because God said so.
When heaven and earth pass away...
We are holy and held by a promise that will never change.
God said so.
Now, we go with the confidence of holy children, sent out to bring out the holiness in each other and in the whole world. Amen.

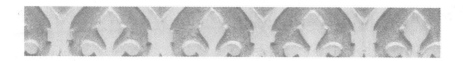

November 21, 2021– Christ the King Sunday

2 Samuel 23:1-7 or Daniel 7:9-10, 13-14; Psalm 132:1-12 (13-18) or Psalm 93; Revelation 1:4b-8; John 18:33-37

LaTrelle Miller Easterling

Preaching Theme

This Sunday marks the last Sunday in the liturgical calendar. When the sun sets on this day, it will conclude another Christian year. Endings provide an opportunity to gaze across the horizon of time to remember what has been and what could have been. Through these reflections, we resolve to live into what should be for all of God's creation.

In this **2 Samuel** text, David looks back over the arc of his life and poetically proclaims that the God who covenanted to be with him from everlasting to everlasting kept that covenant. Conversely, David knows the frailties, failures, and folly of his leadership, and he pours that knowledge into a primer for generations to come. David is the second king to lead the United Kingdom of Israel and Judah. His monarchy was complex, representing some of the best and worst of times. With an honesty that can only come from accountability and repentance, David states without equivocation that leadership in God's name must be just, righteous, and holy. Anything else falls below the privilege and dignity of our salvation. Here, we can ask: Have we taken stock of our record? This Sunday provides an opportunity to do so.

Power comes with the territory of leadership. This is true for leadership both within the church as well as within the larger society. Those who remember the foundation of their power are more likely to use it with humility and restraint. From the Sunday school teacher to the choir director to the lead pastor, those in leadership wield power. Which materials are chosen for the curriculum? Who has the opportunity to sing a solo or even join the choir at all? Who is invited into the pulpit and who is excluded from that sacred space? Each of these decisions is an exercise of power. Were these decisions made in a way that honors God and upholds the life of Christ? Leadership, all leadership, is a gift. How that leadership is lived out before the body of Christ makes a statement and teaches lessons. The same is true for professionals in the larger society. How are they exercising their leadership? Does it honor God? Does it communicate that Christ the King is the Lord of their lives? Does our leadership shine as light, or does it cast darkness?

As we celebrate Christ the King Sunday, the celebration would be devoid of its full impact if we were to limit our experience to pomp and circumstance without substantive introspection. Although Christ is known as our sacrificial Lamb, Christ never sacrificed who he was, what he stood for, or his representation of God—even at pain of death. In light of that model, we must ask ourselves, how much of our lives are lived in contradiction of what we say we believe? One of David's most morally bankrupt actions occurred because he convinced himself no one was looking. When we think no one is looking, what are we doing? This includes the ballot box, our 2:00 a.m. internet browsing, and our support of unethically made products, as well as a host of other actions. Our faith becomes disembodied when we compartmentalize our lives into the sacred and the secular. The concluding verses of this scripture warn of what awaits those who ignore David's farewell sermon.

Sermon Extras

Seeking Holiness

In our current milieu, dreams are typically associated with obtaining success or achieving a goal. We encourage our youth and young adults to follow their dreams. We buoy our self-doubt by reminding ourselves that the distance between our dreams and our reality is the sweat of our brow or the discipline of our mind. Within the Western culture and mindset, dreams are a private affair and sometimes they are even dismissed pejoratively as childlike fantasies. To dream is to imagine what could be achieved, often for personal gain. But in the ancient world, dreams were understood as a means of communication between the heavenly and the earthly realm. In the Book of **Daniel**, the prophet experiences dreams that foretell an epic battle between the forces of good and the forces of evil. This dream is not given to Daniel for private purposes; rather, it is for the sake of the community.

There is an opportunity to reclaim our deep mystical roots. Mysticism is often disregarded as antiquated or misunderstood as a sound Christian foundation. However, Richard Rohr reminds us that mysticism is simply moving from mere belief to an actual inner experience of God. John Wesley's Aldersgate experience opened the portal from head to heart as he physically experienced Christ's saving power. Exploring modern-day prophets and mystics can reawaken the often-neglected practice of contemplative prayer and meditation. Contemporary mystics include people, such as Sojourner Truth, Thomas Merton, Henri Nouwen, and Howard Thurman. Invite the congregation into a regular rhythm of contemplative prayer, centered meditation, and journaling. Invite them to offer their whole beings to God and invite them to proclaim, "God, I offer you even my dreams."

Worship Helps

Call to Worship (Based on Psalm 93)

Great is the Lord, and greatly to be praised!
The Lord rules! The Lord is robed in majesty, clothed with strength!
Great is the Lord, and greatly to be praised!
The Lord set the world firmly in place, it won't be shaken.
Worthy is the Lord; worthy is the name of the Lord!
The Lord's laws are faithful, rooted in justice and righteousness!
Worthy is the Lamb; worthy is the Holy One of Israel!
ALL: The waters roar and the seas wave, but greater is the Lord our God.
   The Lord will reign forever and ever!

A Prayer for Sunday, November 21, 2021

God of the prophets, you have spoken throughout time to, and through, your prophets,
casting a vision for your people,
nurturing them with divine assurances,
empowering them with divine inspiration,
anointing them for holy leadership,
setting them apart for your sacred service.

Speak boldly to your prophets in this present age,
send a fresh anointing upon them to steady
stammering tongues and evict errant wills.
Speak boldly through your prophets in this present age,
send a fresh anointing upon them to suppress
selfish intentions and rebuke godless gain.

Fill their minds and mouths with your divine revelation;
a revelation not of this world, but of your divine realm.
Call to them in their dreams.
Call out to the men and women, young and old,
to those who have ears to hear your word from on high.
Call out from the east and west, the north and south,
a unifying word that will
comfort and convict,
dismantle and disturb,
restrict and resurrect,
enable and ennoble,
loose and liberate.

Speak to your prophets, God, that your people may be
filled and fed,
loved and led. Amen and amen.

November 25, 2021–
Thanksgiving Day

Joel 2:21-27; Psalm 126; 1 Timothy 2:1-7; Matthew 6:25-33

Jennifer and Todd Pick

Preaching Theme

My son's first word was *uh-oh*, which was troubling enough. His second word was *mine*. "Mine!" he would triumphantly declare as his chubby fingers clutched whatever toy or food was before him. There is a glorious amount of power in the thought of possession, even for our littlest ones, who can claim ownership over so few things in their young lives. We learn this word, *mine*, so early in life that the desire to obtain, control, or simply have the things we want never truly goes away. Thanksgiving Day, however, has a way of reminding us that this is not how things work in God's economy.

On a day when we pause from our daily routines to count our blessings around tables of abundance, we might also pause and ponder that there is actually very little over which we can claim absolute ownership. Our festive celebrations on Thanksgiving Day come with a startling reality: nothing we have is truly ours. In Hebrew there is no verb for *to have*, as in *to possess*. The expression we translate into English as *to have* (*yesh li*) more accurately means something like "it is there to me," or "there is available to me." When we assess what we "have" and what is "mine" in this light, perhaps we can better see that nothing really *belongs to us*. Instead, everything is *made available to us from God* and is simply *on loan to us for a time*.

During this glorious time of harvest, nature's fruitfulness helps us understand just how much is available to us. The cycle of gratitude, of release and return, is on grand display before us. Just like the leaves that have turned and returned to the earth, there's a whisper on the autumn winds calling us to release our hearts to the winds of the Spirit and return them to God once again. In the abundance of fruit and grain brought in from the field is another reminder to return our lives to God so that we might bear fruit for the kin-dom, becoming a harvest of righteousness and peace.

As we lift our praise and participate in this cycle of gratitude, release, and return, we begin to remember that we do not own the earth and its fullness and fruitfulness. What has been brought in from the field should help us remember that we belong to the earth; that we should borrow only what we need from it. In this season in which we practice giving thanks and returning a portion of what we have borrowed—what has been on loan to us—we acknowledge God's abundant gifts and all that has been entrusted to our care.

As we offer our thanks and praise in community, many of us will be asked to participate in interfaith services. Giving thanks to God is an action upon which we all can agree. In such services, it might be wise to focus on the wealth contained in our Hebrew scriptures. **Psalm 126** is a song of joy! For this pilgrimage, people who owned very little other than their dignity could barely contain their surprise and delight when meeting with better circumstances: "Our mouths were suddenly filled with laughter; our tongues were filled with joyful shouts" (Ps 126:2a). These pilgrims knew that the road that lay ahead was still strewn with cutting rocks, but for that moment in the journey, the hardship eased. They suddenly remembered that grace could be found at any point along the journey. Grace, unexpected and undeserved, washed over them. Their tears watered both their parched souls and the desert land, which they knew would produce a harvest of joyful shouts and grain.

Secondary Preaching Themes

The scripture from **Joel** seems to declare a promised future that the psalmist sings of in the present. The people of God move in and out of favor, through wilderness and promised land, under empires and despotic kings. Yet, when they find a small fraction of unexpected grace, they sing, as the psalmist does, in community. Perhaps in this season of thanksgiving, we can learn from this practice as well. Perhaps we focus less on what we will eat or what we will wear and turn our attention to the birds and the lilies from **Matthew's** Gospel, remembering how much God cares for all of creation. It is so easy to turn our lamenting gaze to what we lack at the moment. Thanksgiving and the cycle of gratitude, release, and return pattern our hearts to recognize that everything has been made available to us for a time, to give thanks, and to sing the song of harvest home.

Worship Helps

Gathering Prayer

God of sowing and harvesting, we lift our thanks and praise for the cycles and seasons that remind us of your faithfulness, your generosity, and the abundance of your love. Thank you for walking with us through all the seasons of life. We come today, remembering the moments in which you have restored us from despair to laughter, from sadness to joy, from fear to gladness. We come today, remembering that all we have comes from you. In our rejoicing and remembering, let gratitude reorient our hearts that we might live in grateful praise always. Amen.

Call to Worship

Like grain from the field, gather your people, O God.
Gather us around your table of life!
Like fruit from the vine, gather your people, O God.
Gather us into your feast of love!
With many hearts gathered as one,
gather us into your heart of holiness!
With many voices gathered as one,
gather us into your song of thanksgiving!
Gather your people, O God.
Gather us into your arms and hold us forever!

Benediction

With seeds of joy to sow in deserts of despair:
we go, in thanksgiving, with God the sower.
With seeds of hope to sow in valleys of shadow:
we go, in thanksgiving, with Christ our light.
With seeds of possibility to sow in trenches of tears:
we go, in thanksgiving, with the Spirit of life.
Go now, in thanksgiving, bearing seeds for sowing
so that all might come home with shouts of joy.
Thanks be to God! Amen.

An Advent Sermon

"Like It or Not, God's Redemption" [1]
by Will Willimon

Jeremiah 33:14-16; Luke 21:25-28

"There will be signs in the sun, moon, and stars. On the earth, there will be dismay among nations in their confusion over the roaring of the sea and surging waves. The planets and other heavenly bodies will be shaken, causing people to faint from fear and foreboding of what is coming upon the world. Then they will see the Human One coming on a cloud with power and great splendor. Now when these things begin to happen, stand up straight and raise your heads, because your redemption is near." (Luke 21:25-28)

On the first Sunday of Advent, Jesus always gets weird, not just because he talks about apocalyptic signs in the sun, moon, and stars, but because Jesus speaks of *redemption*—cataclysmic, world-shaking, interventionist, God-wrought redemption.

Do you like it when Jesus talks about redemption? The great Catholic theologian, Flannery O'Connor, had one of her characters, an anti-preacher, famously say, "Any man with a good car don't need redemption."[2] How expensive was the car that brought you here?

It was June 1984, my very first Sunday at Duke Chapel. Durham was doing its seasonal nosedive into drought, turning West Campus into the Sahara. So, during the Prayer of Intercession, I prayed for rain: "Lord, we beseech thee, send us rain. We promise to be good if you'll send us rain. Please, make it rain."

Then, this professor accosted me after service: "Praying for rain? Duke Chapel is a sophisticated, thoughtful, university church!" Harrumph.

On my second Sunday at a sophisticated, thoughtful, university church, the day's gospel was about Jesus feeding the multitudes with a few loaves and fish. Afterwards, an earnest sophomore jumped me. "How can you preach on hunger without once urging us to organize to fix the problem of hunger? That was irresponsible!" *A sophomore calling me irresponsible?*

"The gospel was about Jesus, not better food distribution. If you know how to 'fix world hunger' why are you wasting time here in church?"

Thus I was unsurprised when, in a survey of what you expect from my sermons, you said, "I want a sermon that reminds me of my Christian responsibility and then motivates me to use my talents to respond to the needs of the world."

OK. You asked for it. Write this down. Get that tiny golf pencil from the pew rack and write this down! *Church: this week you must do something about your sexism, racism, classism, ageism, and ethnocentrism. Stop using Styrofoam, go vegan, gluten free, eat locally, think globally. If you want peace, then work for justice; fight against gentrification; don't drink so much; don't give so little; practice civility, mindfulness, and inclusiveness; and take precautions on dates! Keep the Sabbath, breathe deeply, live simply, practice diversity, and perform random acts of kindness. You drink too much!*

Don't you give me that look when I'm in the midst of moralizing! *Do a good deed daily; first, be sure you're right, then go ahead; love your neighbor as yourself. It's up to you to do right, or right won't be done. You are the hope of tomorrow, you can do anything you set your mind to. You drink too much!*

Notice anything missing?

God.

Come back next Sunday; I'll give you another list. You are responsible, sensitive, caring, compassionate, liberal, open-minded, culturally diverse, gluten-free, mindful people who have your master's degrees—otherwise you wouldn't be coming to this church. Christianity is a kind of primitive, Jewish technique for motivating responsible people (like us) to do what we need to do to save ourselves by ourselves.

You think you are a good person who is making progress. Pelagians come to church for moral fine-tuning, not for redemption. They come for a bit of a spiritual boost, not the Son of Man rending the heavens and coming down to rip apart the cozy arrangements we have made with the status quo. We're looking for a gentle confirmation of our better angels, not God-wrought, world-disrupting redemption.

Sorry. It's the first Sunday of Advent and (did you notice?) *none of today's texts are about you.* There's nothing in any of today's scriptures about what you should think, feel, or do.

I know that makes you uncomfortable.

Advent delights in rubbing our noses in scripture that makes people like us nervous, people who have advanced degrees, drive Volvos, shop at Whole Foods, and eat kale. Relax. Advent doesn't apply to you. Advent is for other people; it's for people who can't save themselves, people who don't even have the boots to pull themselves up by their own bootstraps, people who find the political and economic deck stacked against them, people who've got no hope... *but God.*

I trusted you! You told me you were progressive, enlightened people making moral progress, getting your acts together, monitoring your gluten intake and your drinking. And then, just a couple of Advents ago, you snuck into a dark booth, closed the curtain, and when nobody was looking, elected a serially-adulterous, casino owning, prevaricating...!

I don't think I'll ever trust you again with the fate of the whole world.

Oh, we have good intentions. We get organized, take action, vote, and send troops to our border to protect us from pregnant women... and end up putting more of our fellow citizens in jail than any country in the world.

All we wanted to do was to provide security for our families... and thereby, we created the most violent country in the world. We wanted privacy, and we got loneliness. Fashioning freedom, we unintentionally enshrined inequity.

We are just the sort of people who, one Friday afternoon—democracy in action, power to the people, church and state cooperating, biblical fidelity, making Judea great again—just happened to torture God's Son to death on a cross.

A sermon is not about you. A sermon is about *God*. When we read and then preach scripture, we pray for the guts to ask dangerous, but potentially redemptive questions, such as: *Who is God? What's God up to now? How can we hitch on to what* God *is doing?*

You said you sincerely wanted to do better, you said that you craved my sanctimonious advice on how you could set yourself, and the world, aright. Then you went and messed everything up by being... *human, finite, mortal, sinful,* just the sort of reprobates Jesus loves to redeem.

Wherein is our redemption, if it's not in ourselves? All of this morning's scripture has a theme: *God is coming.* Or as we say it in church-speak: Advent.

Though time and time again we have shown our inability to go toward God, there is good news: *God is moving toward us.*

We've got a God who loves to redeem the worst of times into God's good time. Jeremiah says that God has given up waiting for us to reform our politics. God's going to send us a new King of David, a president who will "execute judgment and righteousness in the land" since we can't (Jer 33:15 KJV). Jesus foretells, "signs in the sun, the moon, and the stars, and on the earth distress among nations confused by the roaring of the sea and the waves... [by which we will see] 'the Son of Man coming'... with power and great glory... your redemption is drawing near" (Luke 21:25-28 NRSV).

I personally believe that we are living in one of the saddest seasons for American democracy. Some of it is not Donald Trump's fault. But how do I know what time it is? With a redemptive God, you never know if it's Good Friday or Easter. As Jesus says in today's gospel, when the sky turns dark and the stars fall (bad news), look up! Your redemption is drawing nigh.

Good news or bad? I guess it depends on how scared you are of the possibility of a living, active, interventionist, judging, creating, destroying, loving... God.

Or maybe good news or bad news depends on how badly you need a God who does for you what you can't do for yourself.

The highlight of worship, in my thousands of Sundays in Duke Chapel, was not my sermon, of course. It was Communion, the Eucharist, when I got to watch you come forward and hold out your empty hands, just like little children, to receive the mystery of the body and the blood of Christ.

I know you have achieved much, that you are good at knowing and fixing things. But in that potentially redemptive moment, when you held out your empty hands, needy, unselfconsciously as a little child, like a beggar, like you just couldn't go on without being given a gift that you couldn't earn, well, that was as good as it gets in this church. You at your most truthful and God at God's most redemptive.

It's Advent. Keep your eye on the sky. Get ready to be redeemed, like it or not.

Advent Sermon Series

Tanya Linn Bennett

Introduction for Advent Sermon Series

The holy seasons offer a unique opportunity to introduce a sermon series relating the scripture readings for the time to each other and to the experience of journeying toward the high event. Advent offers a particularly unique opportunity for this type of series. I've written four settings for preaching and worship for this Advent time based on these themes: waiting, watching, wanting, and wondering. Although these are not the traditional weekly themes, most often recalled as hope, joy, peace, and love, these themes invite us into introspection, reflection, and preparation.

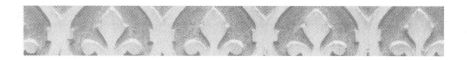

November 28, 2021– First Sunday of Advent

Jeremiah 33:14-16; Psalm 25:1-10; 1 Thessalonians 3:9-13; Luke 21:25-36

Tanya Linn Bennett

Preaching Theme: Waiting

Both of the **Luke** and **Jeremiah** texts speak to the nature of waiting. In both texts, the people are waiting for an apocalyptic moment to arrive. And, in both cases, the stories seem to unfold out of order. As Jeremiah declares to the people that God's promise is real, that a righteous branch will be lifted up to save the people, the armies of Nebuchadnezzar, king of Babylon, are advancing toward Jerusalem. It won't be long before bodies lie in the street, families are destroyed, and violence surrounds God's people. And yet, there is this promise lying beyond the devastation, that Judah will be saved and that the people of Jerusalem will live in safety. The Gospel of Luke equally offers a vision of the very planet itself rising up against the people. Tsunamis and floods, signs in the skies among the constellations, and earthquakes, all shaking people into a fear and foreboding about what is happening to the very world that they have known and understood. It is important to note, here, that the word translated into English as *world* is not the word for a physical planet, but for a governmental structure and economic system. Despite the description of the natural world rising up against the people, it is this sociopolitical *world* that will be torn apart in the days to come. Perhaps it is the natural world pushing against this unjust, human-constructed world that is God's workforce in this story.

In both cases, the people must wait. They must wait, first for the impending disaster and then for God's redemptive promise to arrive. In general, people aren't experts at waiting, particularly when it means living through agony to get to the good life. But the writer of Luke is aware of the human tendency to self-medicate, to anesthetize, and to quell our big anxieties with the distraction of small worries. The people are to stay alert, praying with all they've got, so that they are fortified enough to survive the disasters to come, so that they will be ready to receive the promised one, the living branch, the one riding on the clouds and to receive their redemption.

These are not necessarily texts that our faithful people in the pews want to hear in the first week of the Advent season. The waiting we want to do in this season is a kind of waiting that does not need to survive an apocalypse to receive the promised

Holy Child, Prince of Peace, Lord of light. But the reality is, we already live in this apocalypse. We live in a world that is melting around us, dissolving under the weight of supporting a people who have not paid attention to the natural world as we developed our political, economic, and military systems. We live in a world where violence against people based on xenophobia is rife. We live in a world where children are the most regular victims of warfare, homelessness, poverty, and sexual abuse. We live in this apocalyptic world already, so the hopefulness of waiting is in knowing that redemption and justice will arrive. And, it's in our waiting with righteousness, alertness, and patience, that we participate in its arrival.

Sermon Extras

Seeking Holiness

We don't often practice waiting, or simply sitting still. In small groups of four to five people, after each Advent Sunday worship, gather in a corner of the sanctuary, the narthex, the choir lofts, the chancel, or any area within easy reach of the primary worship space and simply stand in silence. The congregational leader will set a timer, each Sunday extending the time (perhaps start with three minutes, then five minutes, and so on). Stand in small circles, breathing together, perhaps holding hands or touching shoulders, in silence and practicing waiting. When the timer disrupts the silence, the congregational leader may close the session with a simple blessing, "Go in peace to bless the world." At a final congregational session, invite a dialogue discussing the impact and effects of standing in communal silence and waiting, and how these have impacted the worshipping community. This practice can be repeated each week during the Advent season, with each session focused on the theme of the day.

Worship Helps

Gathering Prayer

God of us all, keep us strong for this season of waiting, for this season of waiting that calls on us to be courageous in the face of adversity, be hopeful in the face of deep concern, and to be faithful even as the world around us challenges us to distraction.

Opening Sung Prayer

For the beginning of this first Sunday in Advent service, consider opening with a song of prayer, such as, "While We are Waiting, Come," which is found in the *African American Heritage Hymnal*. This simple, lilting song offers a compelling plea to God to send the Holy One while we wait.

Call to Worship

In our silence, is our faithful waiting.
ALL: In our silence, we wait. [Pause.]
In our silence, is our courageous waiting.
ALL: In our silence, we wait. [Pause.]
In our silence, is our hopeful waiting.
ALL: In our silence, we wait. [Pause.]

Benediction

We wait.
ALL: We wait alertly.
We wait.
ALL: We wait patiently.
We wait.
ALL: We wait together.
ALL: Come, Jesus, our Emmanuel, come.

December 5, 2021–Second Sunday of Advent

Baruch 5:1-9 or Malachi 3:1-4; Luke 1:68-79; Philippians 1:3-11; Luke 3:1-6

Tanya Linn Bennett

Preaching Theme: Watching

These two minor prophets often only appear during the Advent season, so what a great opportunity to explore them with your congregation. "Get up, Jerusalem!" the writer of **Baruch** cries out, "Stand on the high place, and look to the east! See your children gathered from the west to the east by the holy one's word, as they rejoice that God has remembered them" (5:5). This is a call not only to watch but also to watch with expectation that God has remembered the people of Israel, the people of Jerusalem. This is so compelling and exciting that we must engage these words and share them. What does it mean to watch with expectation?!

And then **Malachi** tempers that expectation. Yes, God has remembered us, and God sends one to make things right, one who brings justice and righteousness, and one who needs to clear away some of the mess that God's beloved people have made of things in order to make things right. As Malachi says, "Who can endure the day of his coming? Who can withstand his appearance? He is like the refiner's fire or the cleaner's soap. He will sit as a refiner and a purifier of silver" (3:2-3). This is no meek and mild savior. This is one who comes to divide, devastate, and destroy—all so that something new can come.

As Dietrich Bonhoeffer preached in his 1928 sermon:

It is very remarkable that we face the thought that God is coming, so calmly, whereas previously peoples trembled at the day of God....We have become so accustomed to the idea of divine love and of God's coming at Christmas that we no longer feel the shiver of fear that God's coming should arouse in us. We are indifferent to the message, taking only the pleasant and agreeable out of it and forgetting the serious aspect, that the God of the world draws near to the people of our little earth and lays claim to us. The coming of God is truly not only glad tidings, but first of all frightening news for everyone who has a conscience.[1]

So, as we watch for the arrival of the Holy One, Emmanuel, we must also watch our own expectations and assumptions. The Prince of Peace comes to fire things up, not calm things down. This season of preparation invites us to watch with the expectation that this one who comes for all of God's people comes as a force for change, a force of love that will call us all to something different, something new, something unexpected so that God's justice, mercy, and joy can come forth.

Sermon Extras

Seeking Holiness

Building on the first week's small group exercise, offer a timed session in small groups, focusing on the notion of watching. Following the instructions listed under the entry for the first week of Advent, have the small groups gather in corners of the worship space, increasing the time this week. They might reread the verses of the **Baruch** text, focusing on watching as they stand in silent reflection.

Worship Helps

Gathering Prayer

God of us all, we watch and wait. We look east and west, watching for the promised approach of the one the prophets speak of, the one the gospel stories describe, the one who is you with us. Keep us alert and awake, ready to receive the one who comes.

Call to Worship

We look east, faithfully watching.
ALL: We look east, and watch.
We look east, courageously watching.
ALL: We look east, and watch.
We look east, hopefully watching.
ALL: We look east, and watch.

December 12, 2021–Third Sunday of Advent

Zephaniah 3:14-20; Isaiah 12:2-6; Philippians 4:4-7; Luke 3:7-18

Tanya Linn Bennett

Preaching Theme: Wanting

This passage from **Zephaniah** echoes those of the other prophets read in this Advent season with the promise of restoration and elevation of the people of Israel, God's chosen people: "At that time, I will bring all of you back, at the time when I gather you. I will give you fame and praise among all the neighboring peoples when I restore your possessions and you can see them—says the LORD" (3:20). Clearly, this is a time for which the people have waited and watched and, indeed, for which they have longed. The season of Advent points to the heightened anxiety and yearning for salvation, for restoration, and for exaltation of a people who have lived in the shadows for generations, wanting a time of abundance and desiring a time of health and well-being. Zephaniah reminds them of God's promise to gather them back into a nation, restoring them to a place of honor among the neighboring lands, offering to give back what they will need to flourish.

In the United States, and in many lands around the world, we live in nations that could also be restored to a time of well-being and well-meaning, of honor and justice. We desire a restoration, a new creation, or a way of living into God's promise of abundance for all God's people. We desire a time when we can be free from the violence, hegemony, and xenophobia that divides us. We desire the promise of salvation from our own human desires, yearning for God's means of justice and peace. Again, this is spoken of during this holy Advent season. Where do we see the places around us in which this possibility emerges? How do we name this wanting as we watch and wait? **Isaiah** reminds us that "you will draw water with joy from the springs of salvation" (12:3). The question might be for us: Is this a personal salvation or a communal salvation that gathers us up as God's people and offers all of us, everyone, the chance for abundance and well-being? As we wait, watch, and want this Advent season, we find rest in the promise of God with us, Emmanuel.

Sermon Extras

Seeking Holiness

Continuing the small group exercise, gather the groups in corners of the worship space. With the timer in place, ask participants to consider what they desire in this Advent season, what is the deep wanting of their hearts. When the reflection time concludes, invite them to share with each other before concluding in prayer.

Worship Helps

Gathering Prayer

Loving, gracious God, while we wait and watch, we long for you. We want to draw nearer to you. We yearn for the presence of the promised one. In our anxious wanting, calm our desire with your peace and grace. In your precious name we pray.

Call to Worship

We lift our hands toward the springs of salvation, faithfully wanting.
ALL: We lift our hands and want.
We lift our hands toward the springs of salvation, desperately wanting.
ALL: We lift our hands and want.
We lift our hands, hopefully wanting.
ALL: We lift our hands and want.

December 19, 2021–Fourth Sunday of Advent

Micah 5:2-5a; Luke 1:46b-55 or Psalm 80:1-7; Hebrews 10:5-10;
Luke 1:39-45 (46-55)

Tanya Linn Bennett

Preaching Theme: Wondering

What were you doing when you were twelve or thirteen years old?

I can vaguely remember the trauma and triumph of surviving each day of middle school, wondering if I could navigate the social scene and academic landscape. I worked hard in classes I didn't really care about (or that even scared me—can you say geometry?!) and flew through the classes I loved, like writing, music, and social studies.

But I also remember feeling more than mildly outraged at a world that didn't quite see me yet as a force of nature, as someone who had valid thoughts and well-grounded opinions, as someone who had a reliable possibility, even probability, of making a good choice, or of being capable of having a voice in the many places that mattered to me and impacted my life.

I remember knowing that too many things were wrong in the world. I remember feeling angry about what was wrong and wanting passionately to make a difference, having my parents as role models who were activists for civil rights and women's rights.

And maybe that's why this story of Mary, the blessed mother, is so compelling to me and moves me to such a place of belief and trust. So, there's the young Mary, betrothed at the age of twelve, thirteen, or who knows how old she really is, to Joseph. This is not her decision, the passing of her body, self, and identity from her father to her husband. But she's doing her thing. Getting through the day as best she can—in trauma or triumph. Then a remarkable event occurs: the angel comes (what does that look like?) and declares these words, "Rejoice, favored one! The Lord is with you!" (**Luke 1:28**). Mary was "confused" and did not understand, the writer of Luke says,

> The angel said to her, "Don't be afraid, Mary. God is honoring you. Look! You will conceive and give birth to a son, and you will name him Jesus. He will be great and he will be called the Son of the Most High…and there will be no end to his kingdom." Then Mary said to the angel, "How will this

happen since I haven't had sexual relations with a man?" The angel replied, "The Holy Spirit will come over you and the power of the Most High will overshadow you. Therefore, the one who is to be born will be holy. He will be called God's Son." **(1:30-35)**

And you know what Mary says in response? She says, "I am the Lord's servant. Let it be with me just as you have said" **(1:38)**. Now there are a lot of things Mary could have said to that angel, and this would not be the most obvious. Sometimes, this is read as acquiescent, as submissive, but I think that's because Mary saves the good stuff for her cousin Elizabeth. It's when she greets her also impossibly pregnant cousin, Elizabeth, that Mary says why, without protest, she absolutely steps up, or into, the situation. In all of her adolescent agency, with all of her outrage and passion at the insanity happening all around her, she can liberate herself by making her own decision.

As Mary said, let it be according to your word, because this is the wonder of this season. This is the wonder that leads us to do extraordinary, impossible things. This is the wondering that makes us believe that the best good can happen. Mary is a force of nature and she knows it. And this is the gist of what she says to Elizabeth:

God has shown the power of God's promise to the people. God will lift up the lowly and tear down the proud and haughty. God will feed the hungry and send the callous, rich ones away "empty-handed." God will pull the victims of abuse and violence out of the sucking mud of inhumane and oppressive practices and restore them as the beloved ones. And God has chosen *me*, a brown-skinned, adolescent girl who is overlooked, overworked, and betrothed to be Joseph's wife as the vehicle to make this happen. (Based on **Luke 1:46-55**)

Despite the threat of Joseph's rejection and despite the possibility of being stoned to death for being an unwed mother, Mary perseveres. Mary persists. She persists because this wonder-filled thing won't wait for the convenient moment.

This may all seem a little irrational, even delusional, but isn't that what faith in this God and this savior is? It's a trust, an understanding, a confidence that wonder, in its eschatological power, brings forth a new beginning. Could Mary's impetuous, fearless claiming of God's claim on her be a liberating force, for her own self and for so many of us? Could Mary's impetuous, fearless claiming of God's claim on her be contagious this Advent season? Could it take hold of us so that we would also be so bold as to claim God's claim on us, a claim that might call us to do some pretty outrageous and unusual things? If so, it is because wonder will guide us there.

Sermon Extras

Seeking Holiness

Continuing with the post-worship small group exercise, gather in the corners of the worship space to consider the nature of wonder during this Advent season. When the timed reflection session has concluded, invite participants to share what they are "wonder-ing" about this Advent season, and to share what that wonder might lead them to explore, consider, change, or do in the new year.

Worship Helps

Gathering Prayer

Loving God, Holy One, we wait, watch, want, and wonder as the miracle of the arrival of the Christ child approaches again. Open our eyes wide to behold the wonderful birth of the one you send. Prepare our hearts to receive your gift. Amen.

Congregational Prayer

Rather than, or in addition to, the Lord's Prayer, invite the congregation to recite a prayer based on the Hail Mary with confidence, which is something that we don't usually recite in the Protestant tradition, as a remembrance of the wonderful power of the blessed mother, Mary.

Hail, Mary, full of grace, The Lord is with you. Blessed are you among people who are mothers and blessed is the fruit of your nurturing. Holy Mary, bearer of God, pray for us sinners now and forevermore. Amen.

Call to Worship

We look to the angels, faithfully wondering.
ALL: We look to the angels and wonder.
We look to the angels, courageously wondering.
ALL: We look to the angels and wonder.
We look to the angels, impetuously wondering.
ALL: We look to the angels and wonder.

December 24, 2021– Christmas Eve

Isaiah 9:2-7; Psalm 96; Titus 2:11-14; Luke 2:1-14 (15-20)

LaTrelle Miller Easterling

Preaching Theme

The season of Advent gives way to Christmastide. By this time, the greens have been hung in the sanctuary and the home. The rounds of festive caroling in neighborhoods and nursing homes will have been enjoyed. Prayerfully, the manger will remain intact and the cookie swap will experience record-breaking participation. The Advent wreath will be aglow and the "Hallelujah" chorus will still be resonating in the atmosphere. It is Christmas Eve. Again.

While this is often the evening of Lessons and Carols, or of much-anticipated children's plays, it also offers an opportunity for the pastor to transcend the traditional liturgy and plumb the depths of this high, holy season. In a world constantly wrestling with injustice, abuse, tyranny, and global displacement, hearing a powerful message of justice and equality is good news. A careful exegetical analysis of the **Isaiah** text culls the political reality that burdens the citizens in Isaiah's time. At the time, political power had placed the yoke of oppression around the people's necks, and their future seems bleak. The prophet reminded them that their God had not forgotten them. Rather, their God was sending a force greater than darkness to shine a primordial light. What are the parallels between this text and our world? Where do we find the boots of thundering warriors quaking the ground?

I read a blog recently in which a Palestinian Christian surprisingly found herself becoming enraged. As she saw pictures of friends on Facebook who had completed Holy Land tours, she realized they had visited her country without ever really visiting her country...at least the country as she experienced it. In her assessment, the tourists had been offered prepackaged tours that masked the real conflict present in the area. The plight of half the population had been ignored. Her provocative post raises the question: How many experience the Christmas season as a prepackaged holiday tour, never considering the deeper conflicts and contextual complexity present at the time of Christ's birth? Have we reduced the birth of Christ, God breaking through into history to liberate the captives, to mere consumerism? What forces exist today that obscure the metaphorical light of justice and righteousness?

If we experience the birth of Christ in *chronos* over against *kairos*, we may be satisfied to deck the halls rather than join God's greater purpose of pursuing lasting peace. However, the foretelling of a savior in the Psalter, and through the prophet **Isaiah,** announces one who will bring justice and righteousness, equity and fairness. Beyond the transitory nature of seasonal festivities there is a reason for real celebration. The people celebrate liberation from their oppressors and the dawning of a righteous kingdom. That news deserves to be shouted from the mountains and heralded in the plains.

What does justice look like across the globe or across the street? What does righteousness feel like to the immigrant and the citizen occupying the same soil? If our individual or collective consciousness believes there is a difference, is that difference in keeping with God's breaking into the world to "establish and uphold it with justice and with righteousness from this time onward and forevermore" (Isa 9:7 NRSV)? In his poignant liturgy, *Now the Work of Christmas Begins*, Howard Thurman calls to our remembrance the liberative work we are called to do. Are we celebrating the status quo, or the new world order the Christ Child brings?

If we have all the answers of what Christmas means to the world, then have we really asked the right questions?

O come, o come Emmanuel, and ransom captive Israel!

Sermon Extras

Seeking Holiness

Fasting is not often associated with the season of Advent or Chritmastide. And yet, the Pastoral Epistle of **Titus** invites us to practice restraint in a season of excess. As most of our celebration centers on the advent that occurred at the birth of Christ, Titus evokes a forward focus toward the advent yet to come. During this liminal time, our challenge is to live moral and upright lives within a world tempted by depravity. Too often, godly living is portrayed as austere and joyless. However, the lavish love of God's grace is a reason for celebration, singing, dancing, and shouts of praise.

Although the lectionary excludes the hierarchical categorizations found in the verses preceding our reading, a holistic homiletical analysis will not preach the text in isolation. Great care should be taken to avoid any support for beliefs or practices that celebrate privilege. Rather, there is an opportunity to highlight the countercultural call to celebrate humility and equality. This call from Titus goes beyond an intellectual understanding to the praxis of a just distribution of God's abundance to all. This is an urgent call, even though we often want to push it off as an eschatological phenomenon. Or in the words of Walter Rauschenbusch, "One of the most persistent mistakes of Christian [people] has been to postpone social regeneration to a future era to be inaugurated by the return of Christ."[2] On the contrary, this is our work, in our time, and for our world. The congregation, including the children, could be invited to fast from giving gifts to one another and instead offer their resources to a worthy community outreach. This is the real work of Christmas.

Worship Helps

Opening Prayer

As we sing the carols that rouse our hearts, make us mindful of those whose throats have no song tonight. As we light candles of hope, joy, love, and peace, open our eyes to those who feel hopeless, sorrowful, unloved, and afraid. We are still surrounded by too much darkness. Move us beyond our comfortable celebration. Rekindle your light, the light of justice, in our hearts. O come, o come, Emmanuel, and ransom captive Israel. Amen.

Benediction

Beloved,
Do not be afraid of the darkness, within you is the light of Christ.
So, go confidently into the world to:
love without condition,
exude joy with wild abandon,
live simple lives of peace,
and share the good news that our Savior is born!

December 25, 2021– Christmas Day

Isaiah 52:7-10; Psalm 98; Hebrews 1:1-4 (5-12); John 1:1-14

Heather Murray Elkins

Preaching Theme

Christmas morning is on Saturday this year. The timing of this text means that many congregations will be sleeping in, clocking out, or opening presents. Sunday's coming and the angels' announcement could be delayed without disturbing the peace. But there's an imperative truth worth hearing: "Don't be afraid! Look! I bring good news to you—wonderful, joyous news for all people."

If you are preaching for this Saturday service, be it morning or evening, consider presiding at the Table. Early Methodists in America were once identified as those who didn't celebrate Christmas; the church doors would be closed on Christmas Day. They believed that the holy day had become just a holiday, too encumbered with excessive secular festivities to honor Christ; hence, they fasted from public worship services.

In present holy day or holiday worship patterns, there is room at the inn and at the Table for the sacraments, Communion, and baptism. In many churches, Christmas Eve services are not sacramental opportunities due to congregational traditions or leadership. Christmas Day opens the doors to all who are hungry for the incarnation of Word and Table.

In addition, the congregational remnant who gather for this proclamation may have much in common with these everyday heroes, the shepherds who were keeping watch. These are the "good" shepherds in this narrative, no matter how socially marginalized their roles may have been. They showed up. They kept watch, in snow, in rain, in the heat of day, and in the gloom of night. They kept watch over flocks they didn't own, but were willing to give their lives to protect. They served as caretakers of old and young alike. They kept watch against predators and thieves in an occupied nation of the Roman Empire. The pay was not good; the hours, days, and seasons were long. Yet, they got their reward: come Christmas, they got the good news first. They were eyewitnesses to an extraordinary anthem of angels. They got invited into an intimate encounter with Emmanuel, God with us, the beloved, Jesus.

Jesus, the child, was sheltered in a feeding box for animals. Jesus, the light of the world, was laying in the arms of Mary the blessed, and was guarded by Joseph the dreamer. Jesus, the lowly infant whom a tyrant would try to hunt down and kill. The Roman Empire trembled over the presence of a child, and so this holy human family had to flee for their lives. They crossed the borders into Egypt, immigrated back to the land of Pharaoh (a reverse exodus), and paradoxically found shelter.

It is difficult to discern this text beyond the context of our time and place. As this is being written in July 2019, immigrant infants are being separated from their parents at borders of the United States. Families are fleeing their countries; running, walking, swimming for their lives. They are trying to escape violence, but once they cross the border, no matter how they ask for asylum, babies are being taken from their mothers, fathers, or grandparents' arms. Not only are they being forcibly separated and warehoused, caged, and confined but also they may be separated from their family of origin forever. Our governmental oversight does not match that of the shepherds of this Christmas story. Our government officials do not know the name of each lamb. They do not know where the wolves are waiting. These are not their sheep. They are only hired hands; they will not lay down their lives for these forsaken and broken flocks.

Perhaps things will have changed by the time Christmas comes again. Perhaps there will be lights of liberty as far as the eye can see, too numerous to count, like the stars. Perhaps the shepherds in every congregation will have heard the gospel and put it into practice. Perhaps the imperative truth becomes better than the good news of our time: "Don't be afraid! Look! I bring good news to you—wonderful, joyous news for all people."

In the meantime, what do shepherds do through this season?

They do what shepherds always do: keep watch. Tend the flock. Care for the lambs. Call them by name. Listen for the rustle of angel wings. Expect Emmanuel in unexpected places. Pray for hearts to warm, to grow together, and to break open so that doors will open. Gather at the Table where all are welcomed by the Child of God.

Sermon Extras

Engaging Kids & Doing Justice

An old carol question based on Christina Rossetti's "In the Bleak Midwinter" is the motivation for this reflection or action: "What can I bring Him, poor as I am? If I were a shepherd, I would bring a lamb." Giving gifts to the Christ Child as encountered in the countless children who are refugees is one holy day antidote to this holiday's what-did-I-get addiction. This is especially important as an opportunity to teach a carol that's framed in the voice of a child to children in the congregation and in their larger world. As one English chorister prayer goes, "Grant that what we sing with our lips we may believe in our hearts, and what we believe in our hearts we may show forth in our lives."[3]

Children can be invited to make artwork based on the carol they would have learned during Advent or on Christmas Eve. Images of bringing a heart, a blanket, food, or toys to baby Jesus with a special offering to the UMCOR-Global Migration, Advance# 3022144, would connect the scripture text with, and for, the children. They could then lead the congregation in bringing their drawings and the money they have earned or saved during Advent. If a manger is used for Christmas Eve, it could become the place where the congregation brings these special offerings. It would be important to connect their offerings with Christ's offering for us through participation in Holy Communion.

Worship Helps

Call to Worship

The Light that lightens this world has come.
Christ is the newborn sun for this and every day.
We honor Christ's light in one another,
lifting our hands and our hearts to bless
the Spirit and Giver of light and life
as we sing…

Passing the Peace

Suggested Song: "This Little Light of Mine" (sing one verse).

People turn and honor one another by sharing the sign for light.

Sending the Light

What will you do with this light?
Let it shine.
Should you hide it? Try to keep it safe?
Let it shine!
Will you share it? Is it yours, is it mine?
Let it shine. Let it shine!
Where will the light go when it leaves our hands?
We won't be afraid. Angels remind us that our light returns to the Son.[4]

December 26, 2021–First Sunday after Christmas Day

1 Samuel 2:18-20, 26; Psalm 148; Colossians 3:12-17; Luke 2:41-52

Tanya Linn Bennett

Preaching Theme

We approach the pulpit on this Sunday, the day after Christmas, with a question: What do we offer those who gather that is an expression of our gratitude, our celebration, and our reception again of the One whom God sends to save us and set us free?

I was asking myself this very same question on Christmas Eve a few years ago when I encountered a story written by the great theologian Frederick Buechner. The story recounts Buechner's experience of celebrating Christmas Eve at St. Peter's Cathedral in Rome where the pope celebrated the Mass. He describes the enormous crowd that had gathered, people jostling for the best position to see the pope arrive. Every once in a while, spontaneous singing would burst out—"Adeste Fidelis" and "Heiligen Nacht." Finally, after several hours of waiting, Pope Pius XII entered, carried on the shoulders of the Swiss Guard and sitting on a gold throne. The Guard was dressed in their scarlet uniforms, the pope dressed simply in a white alb and cap. Buechner recalls when thinking back on the pope's appearance:

> That lean, ascetic face, gray-skinned, with the high-bridged beak of a nose, his glasses glittering in the candlelight. And as he passed by me he was leaning slightly forward and peering into the crowd with extraordinary intensity. Through the thick lenses of his glasses his eyes were larger than life, and he peered into my face and into all the faces around me and behind me with a look so keen and so charged that I could not escape the feeling that he must be looking for someone in particular.[5]

Buechner concludes that the pope had not glanced around simply to acknowledge the crowd that had gathered, but had been truly looking, searching for the Christ in each of those who had gathered on that Christmas Eve.

This is truly the miracle of the Christmas season. Not that we celebrate again the birth of the Holy Baby, born first over two thousand years ago, but that we celebrate our opportunity to see the Christ in everyone around us. Christ is alive because

Christ lives in and through us. The light of Christ shines in our faces. Who has been the Christ for you this Christmas season, and how have you honored that Christ figure in your midst?

Sermon Extras

Seeking Holiness

Leave slips of paper and pens or pencils on the pews or on the chairs, or have ushers distribute them as congregants enter the worship space. At the conclusion of the sermon, invite worshippers to write on the papers where, or in whom, they have felt, seen, or experienced the spirit of Christ during the Advent and Christmas season. Collect the papers and create a paper chain, folding the paper so that the writing is on the inside. If your worship space has a Christmas tree, then add the chain to the tree. If not, hang it somewhere visible through the Epiphany season. Save the chain to drape on the cross during Lent, a lasting reminder that Christ is alive because Christ lives in, and through, us.

Worship Helps

During the time of prayer, offer an intercessory prayer for the many cares of the world, perhaps using the setting for intercessory prayer, "Pinning Our Hopes on Jesus," which is found in *Cloth for the Cradle* by the Iona Community Wild Goose Worship Group (p. 54). At the conclusion of the prayer, sing "Star-Child" from *The Faith We Sing* (p. 2095). If the prayer from the Iona Group is not used, the verses of "Star-Child" could be used to guide the focus of concerns voiced during the intercessory prayer.

Gathering Prayer

O Holy One, you call us to see your face in all the faces we seek around us. You remind us that in each one of us is the essence of you. This season, may we search for you in everyone we meet. Emmanuel, it is in your name that we pray.

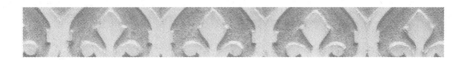

Play It by Ear

**Excerpt from *Simplify the Message: Multiply the Impact*[1]
by Talbot Davis**

Basic Principles of Writing for the Ear

1. **Short sentences.** Your English composition teacher may have been impressed with your compound sentences and your use of the semicolon; your congregation won't be.

2. **Celebrate the vernacular.** Huh? That's a fancy way of reminding you to speak the language of the people to whom you preach. You are preaching for congregants and not for professors. Not even for fellow pastors.

3. **Avoid quotations.** The person sitting in your church is not likely to be as impressed with Bonhoeffer as you are. If you find a quote that is indispensable to the message, hold it up and make a production of reading it (since, after you read the next chapter, the rest of your sermon will be note-less). At Good Shepherd, we had a sermon series coinciding with the two-year anniversary of the racially charged street uprising that rocked our city in 2016. I closed week one of that series by reading *verbatim* this email I had received two years earlier from a parishioner:

On this day when my heart is so very full from sorrow, grief, confusion, and even helplessness as a mother of an African American son, I have to stop and pray and one of the things I prayed for was my church family. I have been attending Good Shepherd for the past five years and was embraced from day one. The moment that I showed up for First Serve for the first time and felt like part of a team that didn't care who I was, where I came from, or if I was a member but was happy I was there and ready to work side by side with me I knew this would be my home church. When my faith starts to waiver, I get a random call from one of the pastors checking on me. When I'm overwhelmed with life I get a call or text out of the blue from a LifeGroup member asking how they can pray for me or how they can serve me that week. When I'm saddened by how my son may be affected by all this, the Nursery Volunteers send me kind notes on how he is a blessing and how much they enjoy having him there. The family of Good Shepherd "get it" and the presence of the Lord is TRULY in this place. Thank you from the bottom of my heart for empowering leaders, inviting all people, and sharing God's word in the midst of unrest and racial tensions in the country. I could easily give up and lose faith but instead my faith and trust in God is stronger than ever and I credit a huge part of that to walking side by side with the people of Good Shepherd.

It was a long quote, of course, but as you might imagine, it was well worth it as we seek to become a "full color" congregation.

4. **Avoid clichés.** As much as you will want to be sparing (but effective) in your use of quotations, you will want to be even more disciplined in avoiding clichés. At the end of the day, avoid clichés like the plague, because when you've seen one you've seen them all, and there are no shortcuts to great writing.

5. **Choose the concrete over the abstract.** Bible college and seminary teach most of us to think conceptually. Terms like *grace*, *repentance*, and *salvation* flow off our tongues. Yet for most of the people to whom we preach, those words remain just that: terms. Concepts. Abstractions. Resist any temptation to define *grace*, for example, by using more words. Instead, define it with a picture, an incident, a metaphor, a demonstration, or a moment when you received something better than you deserve. As I tell people in my preaching workshops, "Don't ever define a word with more words."

In my experience, I write a better sermon when I have confidence in the bottom line to which it points. As I indicated in Chapter One, a rhetorically precise, yet biblically accurate, bottom line is both the great challenge and the true joy of message preparation. I have listed several *types* of bottom lines in that earlier chapter; now let's explore some rules for crafting them to the best of your ability.

Wordsmithing Your Bottom Lines

So you're committed to simplifying your messages and amplifying your impact by zeroing in on one memorable point. Yet before I give some rules I have devised for smithing the words in a bottom line, there are two clear and present dangers along the way.

1. **Mastering the Obvious.** If your bottom line is along the lines of **God loves you** or **Sin has consequences** or **We need to share the Gospel**, well...all of these are TRUE, but none of them are interesting. None of them required getting up for church in the morning because they have been part-and-parcel of church assumptions ever since there was a church. To keep yourself from mastering what is obvious, ask yourself in preparation: "Is this not only true but also interesting?"

2. **Trite Exhortation.** I once heard a radio sermon delivered by a well-respected pastor in which the bottom line was **Don't shirk hard work**. In addition to misusing the text involved—the parable of the talents in Matthew 25—that particular bottom line managed to master the obvious while also using a negative exhortation. And while rhyming. The result was trite...almost juvenile. I long for bottom lines that are neither predictable nor elementary, but are instead provocative, compelling, and *well worded*. How does that happen?

Well-worded bottom lines that capture attention and, most importantly, impact lives, will always stem from the work I described in Chapter Two: exegesis that delights and the joy of discovery that accompanies it. Once it is clear to your congregation that you have been captured by the biblical text, you will have much greater ability to capture their attention. You have been interestED and so are now prepared to be interestING.

With that foundation settled, here are some ways I have found to "smith" the words in a bottom line:

Wordplay

Some of the most effective bottom lines take shape when the preacher plays with the words involved. The kind of wordplay I am talking about includes double meanings, using the same term as both noun and verb, and upending the congregation's expectations. Here are a few examples:

In a message on *kindness* from the *Fashion Statement* series based on Paul's virtue list in Colossians 3:12: **Kindness does for people who can't do for you.**

From a message drawing from James 2 and its discussion of preferential treatment for wealthy church guests: **The favorites you play play you.**

I opened the *Eye Rollers* series with a message on Matthew 5:44, "But I say to you, love your enemies and pray for those who harass you" that landed at this bottom line: **The only way to love your enemies is to realize you're the loved enemy.** Romans 5:10 provided supplemental insight for that one. In that same series I also preached on Jesus's words regarding anger in Matthew 5:21-26. The conclusion? **Your anger fades when you face the ones you anger.** I heightened the contrast with two poles on the platform, one with a sign representing the noun (Your Anger) and the other the verb (You Anger).

Our *Behind the Scenes* series based on the book of Esther launched with a message called "Control Freak, Meet Trophy Wife." The bottom line, inspired by King Xerxes's antics in Chapter One, went this way: **People control you when they can't control themselves.**

During *On the Up and Up*—a series on the Songs of Ascent (Psalms 120–134)—the sermon on Psalm 122 built to **Having the right doesn't give you the right.** That sermon with that bottom line also happened to be delivered on the Sunday closest to the Fourth of July.

From a series called *Only Human*, I developed this bottom line for a sermon on Psalm 8: **It's no accident that you're on purpose.**

My earliest inspiration for sermonic wordplay came, not surprisingly, from an Andy Stanley message from Proverbs: *Wise people know what they don't know.* Simple, compelling, convicting, and memorable. May all your wordplays get the same reviews!

Contrast

One of the most reliable bottom line structures involves contrast. The *best* contrasts expose conventional wisdom for the fallacy it (usually) is, while replacing it with the counterintuitive truth of the Gospel.

In the "For the Gospel" message drawn from Galatians 2:11-21, I drew this contrast: **Heaven isn't a reward for those who are better. It's a gift for those who've been bought.**

In the *Solutionists* series (which became the Abingdon release *Solve*), the lesson I drew from Nehemiah's worker list in Chapter Three (a list that is, at first glance, mind-numbing and at second glance is soul-lifting) was: **Leaving your mark isn't about what you accomplish. It's about who you influence.**

The *Eye Rollers* series culminated with Jesus's most impossible command of them all in Matthew 5:48: "Therefore, just as your heavenly Father is complete in showing love to everyone, so you must also be complete." What do you do with that? A helpful contrast: **You won't have perfect performance for Jesus but you do have perfect position in him.**

Syllable Symmetry

In recent years, I have realized the power of *syllables*. While that fascination may appear to come from a fascination of minutia—what sane person bothers to count syllables?—when you remember that you're writing for the *ear* and not the *eye*, syllables matter a great deal. People *hear* syllables more powerfully than they read them, and if the impactful preacher learns to use syllables symmetrically, he or she will then preach more memorably. When at all possible, smith your words in such a way that critical terms in the bottom line have the same number of syllables.

Symmetric syllables work especially well on opposing sides of a contrasting statement. Here are some examples:

When you stop pretending you'll start becoming.

What you tolerate today will dominate you tomorrow. (*Tolerate* and *dominate* have a symmetric number of syllables. While *today* and *tomorrow* don't, the natural contrast still helps to implant the line in people's minds.)

Giving isn't your duty. It's your design.

Doubt justifies disobedience, but surrender magnifies understanding.

Alliteration

Let me admit: anytime a preacher alliterates, he or she is potentially walking on thin ice (wait, aren't we supposed to avoid clichés?). We've all heard multi-point sermons in which each of the points began with the same letter. For some reason *P* was the most popular first letter, as in a sermon that walks through Jesus's...

Power

Purpose

Promise

However, in the right hands and used with discipline and restraint, the power of alliteration is undeniable. In particular, the right alliteration can make a sermon's bottom line "percussive"—a sentence that sounds in such a way that it both pops and sticks. For the *For the Gospel* message I referenced above, my original bottom line was: **Heaven is not for the better than. It's for the rescued from.** Good but not memorable...and one that would require at least a couple of sentences of further explanation. So in the process of internalizing and sounding out the sermon (see next chapter), I came up with a bottom line that was much improved because of its alliteration: **Heaven is not a reward for those who are better. It's a gift for those who've been bought.** The contrasting of *better* and *bought* gave it a resonance it would not have had otherwise—while also highlighting the *nothing-but-the-blood* power of the Gospel.

Some other alliterative bottom lines:

Your opposition is just your opportunity in disguise.

What you invent will always tie you up; what you inherit will never let you down.

You won't have perfect performance for Jesus but you do have perfect performance in him.

Prepositions

I have saved my favorite bottom line wordsmiths for last: prepositions. With a slight adjustment to the smallest words, an impactful preacher can both expose the folly of God-less thinking and illumine the beauty of Gospel living. These bottom lines often take the most work to uncover—remember *the more effortless it looks, the more effort it took?*—yet they are deeply rewarding once found. They also have the added benefit of using diction and syntax that *no one* would label confusing or academic. Here are some of the strongest bottom lines that twisted on just a (small) word or two:

From *Lost Hope*, a message that dug into Elijah's death wish and God's provision in 1 Kings 19: **God won't do for you what he needs to do with you.**

I started 2018 with *Practicing the Presence*, a series inspired by Brother Lawrence and focusing on spiritual disciplines. The first sermon came from a survey of Psalms that gives witness to the power of morning prayer. The bottom line: **Where you start the day determines how you finish it.**

The *Crash Test Dummies* series concluded with a survey of Samson, perhaps the least heroic hero in the biblical library. What lesson did we draw from a man whose story ends up literally in a heap of rubble? **Surrender your impulses so you don't surrender to them.** That particular bottom line emerged not only from biblical study but also from pastoral counseling...and now that it has been both *preached* and *published*, it has worked its way back into the counseling room. Often.

Outlaw Words

While we're talking about the intersection of wordsmithing and proclamation, here is a list of words we should outlaw from future sermons. They have been used, misused, and overused to the point that they no longer have meaning—if, in fact, they ever did.

Countless. Unless you're talking about the sands on the seashore or stars in the sky, nothing is really countless. Whether it is the number of people influenced for the Gospel by your favorite preacher (or Billy Graham himself) or the amount of animals your church has blessed in an annual celebration, the number in question is concrete and countable. Don't exaggerate the accomplishment and minimize the truth by labeling it as something it is not.

Amazing. Especially when you draw the syllables out: *Uh-MAY-Zing.* When everything is amazing, nothing is. Except grace.

More than you ever imagined. OK, this one is five words, not one. But the phrase functions as a filler in most sermons. It is guilty of two major sins: (1) it overpromises and underdelivers, and (2) it is vague rather than concrete. Promises that lack precision neither engage nor empower your hearers.

Equivocation (the practice, not the word). We handle the Gospel. It is *good news* and not *average news!* Jesus offers an *abundant life*, not a *mundane one.* To die is to *gain*, not to be *gone.* The people in our churches are used to and annoyed with double speak and half-truths in their daily lives. Let's give them the unabridged Gospel in unequivocal language. As Robert Jacks reminds us: "Consider the words of the preacher who was the supreme equivocator: 'If you don't repent, so to speak, you'll be damned, as it were.'"[2]

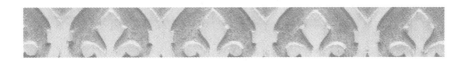

Preacher as Transformational Intellectual

Excerpt from *Preaching to Teach: Inspire People to Think and Act*[1] by Richard W. Voelz

At times the preacher steps into the pulpit with the intent to teach in a traditional sense: the preacher dusts off an old doctrine with fresh language, interprets a difficult passage of scripture, employs the historical-critical method to give contextual background to a scripture, or even gives some perspective on a hot-button topic. It is, after all, what a recent Gallup poll tells us people are seeking. Churchgoers want sermons that (1) teach them more about scripture and (2) help them connect religion to their own lives.[2] Isn't this enough to satisfy our definition of teaching?

The problem with this, of course, is that this produces a rather flat account of the power and potential of preaching. As I write the first draft of this chapter, the tragedy in Charlottesville has occurred. As a result of white nationalism and its insidious anti-Semitism and racism, a thirty-two-year-old woman named Heather Heyer was murdered when protest and counterprotest converged. Just days before, the world looked on as a seeming nuclear standoff between the United States and North Korea unfolded. Only a week or two removed, the monumental hurricanes Harvey and Irma struck—further examples of catastrophic weather events exacerbated by climate disruption. Sandwiched between the two, the DACA program was rescinded, threatening close to a million US-born children of immigrants. Faced with these enormous challenges, merely teaching "more about scripture" in our preaching hardly seems worth the effort.

Of course, preaching can be prophetic, seeking to provoke transformation. But as I said earlier, such prophetic preaching produces anxiety among preachers who feel it necessary to muster the courage to preach prophetically *this Sunday*. Nora Tisdale rightly points to seven resistances to prophetic preaching:

1. An inherited model of biblical interpretation that marginalizes the prophetic dimensions of Scripture

2. Pastoral concern for parishioners

3. Fear of conflict

4. Fear of dividing a congregation

5. Fear of being disliked, rejected, or made to pay a price for prophetic witness

6. Feelings of inadequacy in addressing prophetic concerns

7. Discouragement that our own prophetic witness is not making a difference[3]

Tisdale goes on to note that the aversion to prophetic preaching is not wrong, and that pastors should seek "some sort of balance between the prophetic and the pastoral."[4] Despite helpfully tying together the pastoral and prophetic functions, preachers may still experience a kind of juggling act for their preaching, having to decide when one's preaching ministry has become too prophetic in the eyes of others and not pastoral enough, and vice versa. And this is no less difficult even when the prophetic sermon serves pastoral needs! In my own preaching experience, this kind of constant self-assessment was maddening and perhaps unhealthy. And I wonder just how long preachers can bear the weight of preaching prophetically in their community.

Herein lies the connection to teaching. Rather than having to assess whether our preaching was prophetic enough for our congregation (or our clergy peers!), I propose that we use a different measure, if you will. Or, really, no measure at all. I do not mean that we get to excuse ourselves from self-assessment. Instead, in a fuller account of preaching-as-teaching, preaching that we might have characterized as prophetic no longer falls on a kind of continuum between prophetic or pastoral, or some kind of blend of the two, for which Tisdale makes the case in her book. From my personal experience, this assessment of the pastoral and prophetic dynamic was entirely too anxiety-producing to maintain, especially given the dizzying pace with which catastrophic news events unfold in the digital age. Thus, I contend that preaching-as-teaching through the lens of critical pedagogy can help bear this weight, so to speak, because preaching-as-teaching encompasses more than just giving biblical and theological information to uninformed, mostly passive listeners.

ß

Conclusion

The preacher-as-teacher is a transformative intellectual: not a dry lecturer satisfied to deliver knowledge to passive or ignorant listeners, but rather one who stands before and with the congregation, authorized to publicly interrogate the contested spheres of church and world, taboos, division, and weariness. Preaching-as-teaching provides an intervention in the lives of those who gather, empowering them for critical thought and work toward various kinds of transformation.

This self-conception prompts several questions to be included in each week's sermon preparation process. The following questions are suggestive, but certainly not exhaustive of the kinds of things the preacher-as-teacher might ask:

a) What does my community know, what do they need to know, and how might that knowledge move them toward critical thought and transformation?

b) Is a kind of hegemonic power at work to keep my community of faith at arm's length from a topic or issue and related biblical text(s), or vice versa?

c) Who or what sets the precedent for silence or conflict, and who benefits by keeping it as such?

d) Why does the reinforcement between public-private apply in this situation but not another?

e) How are we implicated or complicit in the outcome of that silence or conflict?

f) How do I reflect on my own preaching practices, and toward what end(s)?

The preacher-as-teacher seeks to bring to light the power structures that are maintained by silence or conflict. Based on the authority granted from various sources, but most notably the gathered congregation, preaching in the mode of the preacher-as-teacher becomes an authorized intervention in a congregation's common life for the purposes of ecclesial imagination, sharing the resources for formation and flourishing, and inviting listeners into ways of life that reflect the realm of God.

Critical pedagogy imagines the role of teaching as those who contribute to the formation of public life. Teaching is a transformative and intellectual activity that acts as a form of cultural politics. Teachers regularly intervene in the lives of students by teaching emancipatory practices rather than formation of skills or preparation for the workforce. Preaching-as-teaching uses the sermon as an exercise in critical thinking to help the faithful exercise agency in and beyond the ecclesial sphere. The preacher-as-teacher preaches with an aim to enable the gathered community to approach the issues at hand with critical thought, then act with emancipatory impulses and courageous love. And all of this with the public sphere in mind.

Getting in Front of the Text

**Excerpt from *Beyond the Tyranny of the Text:
Preaching in Front of the Bible to Create a New World*[1]
by James Henry Harris**

Preaching is an action, bold and often dangerous, and this action is itself a "text." Getting in front of the scripture text is a major part of the action I am talking about. It not only "projects a possible world,"[2] as Ricoeur asserts, but action also has a good chance of creating a world that serves as an alternative to the existing one. For example, I can imagine Rosa Parks rising up and going to the front seat of the bus in Montgomery, Alabama, in 1955. This action of "getting in front" is not simply metaphoric but metonymic—almost literal. The action that I am referring to requires a certain movement on the part of the preacher. The intention of the author may in fact be relevant and important, but it is not decisive.[3] The idea that the text creates a "possible world" is critical here because human possibility is the crux of freedom and transformation.

Conscientious and prophetic Black preachers and laypeople seemed to have believed this long before scholars like Ricoeur put it into words. The slaves, for example, saw possibility and a hope that prevented their extinction and made a way for freedom. Freedom is always only a possibility for the oppressed, and "freedom has always been an expensive thing," as Martin Luther King Jr. reminds us.[4]

Black liberation preaching and theology is all about creating and disclosing a possible world. Now, by getting in front of the text, I mean approaching the text by going through the front door of the scripture text, that is, finding a new contemporary point of entry. The act of getting in front of the text itself is grounded in having a hope and vision for the text that not even the past can control and the text itself cannot predict. To be sure, the text can explode with new meaning and hope, which is a powerful metaphor, but it is also a metonym, meaning that getting in front of the text depends on not being mesmerized by the past history of the text but being transformed by its eschatological future! A future pregnant with possibilities and hope.

It is what the text means now, today, in your context and congregation, that matters most. It is what the text says now that is important, not the finite horizon of the text's author that determines the contemporary meaning of the text. That is up to the intellectual creativity of the preacher. We have to extend the career of the text by getting in front of it every time we get a chance to use it as a foundation for the sermon—breaking it away from the tight grip of authority claimed by its author, who no longer has any real practical authority on the text. The text has a new interpretation now, a new meaning that the preacher has given it by getting in front of it.[5]

As a Black preacher in America, reading is a critical act of freedom. For example, I am a part of a tradition that includes the evil experience of chattel slavery where learning to read in the English language was forbidden and punishable by death. I can still feel some semblance of its effects languishing in my collected subconscious. This is not my exclusive story because my own personal history and the history of others also help to constitute this tradition. I cannot escape the historical experience of the past—a past deeply rooted in suffering and highly correlated with the excess of evil perpetuated against a people whose only crime was the color of their skin. Reading is key to staying connected to past history and escape its debilitating effects when necessary.

Now this is where history and distanciation are incommensurate. There is no aesthetic or spiritual distance between slavery and myself, in the sense that every day I see in my mind's eye the bruising evils of slavery as I walk down the pathways of the James River and drive down Route 460 through Prince George, Sussex, Waverly, and Ivor, into the vicinity of Franklin and Southampton County, Virginia, where slave preacher Nat Turner died at the hands of the architects of the slavocracy. I can hear the echo of the Marabai, the echo of bloodhounds chasing the Black body. And I can see in my mind's eye the fear and the pain in the eyes of the slave women and men as they faced the despotic and demonic sovereign power of the evil slave master.

These haunting memories are instantiated in my being and mitigate against distanciation. This anamnesis is a recurring mimesis for me. What I mean here, is that memory continues to repeat or represent itself over and over again. Yes, there is clearly some space of time and place between then and now, but this is a past that is not dead for me. It is a sublation of death. This suffering survives the sting of death. It is "not even past," as William Faulkner says, because it haunts me and boggles my mind and spirit every single day. This is a type of torture that never escapes the Black conscious mind and body. This is the dilemma and crisis of the Black preacher in particular, and the conscious preacher in general.

Reading the Text

As a preacher, before you do anything else, you begin the sermon preparation process by choosing and settling on a scripture text. If you can read, then you can preach, but you have to have a text. No scripture text means no sermon. You may have a form of written discourse, but it is not even headed in the direction of a sermon. The text precedes a topic or title of a sermon. The title of the sermon grows out of the scripture text, not the other way around. So, choose the text first! You do this by reading and studying a little every day—not in search of something to preach but in search of feeding your soul, mind, and spirit. This approach will keep you from scrambling on Saturday and, God forbid, trying to get a sermon together on Sunday morning! The sermon needs time to marinate and seep into the pores of your body and soul. And it needs prayer, which should be an integral part of reading.

After settling on a scripture text for the foundation of the sermon, I recommend reading the chosen text in at least five different English translations such as the New

Revised Standard Version (NRSV), the New International Version (NIV), the Good News Bible, the King James or New King James Version (KJV/NKJV), and the Living Bible or Message Bible, which are more of an interpretation or loose translation. These different renderings of the text should allow the reader to make comparisons and detect minor or major differences in the translated text. Keep in mind that all translations are at least partially subjective because they make an axis through the experience of those doing the translating. There is no pure objective translation because human beings are impure subjective entities with biases, emotions, preferences, distinct personalities, and prejudices. All of these human psychological traits tend to make their way into the original translation of the Greek or Hebrew text as well as into the modern translated English Bible.

After reading the text in five or six versions (or as many versions as is deemed reasonable), the preacher should then try to get a good *sense* of the text. This is what I call a first sense of the text, a "naïve sense,"[6] and an even more naïve understanding of the text. Here we experience the sheer or pure "pleasure of the text."[7] This is the prelude to a full understanding of the text that manifests itself aesthetically as a mental and physical feeling for the text or a textual aestheticism. This is a spiritual and emotional connection with the text—a chasing after its meaning. This process can be construed as a type of textual ecstasy that will lead to the development of a powerful textual sermon. But, as I said, the preacher has to lose herself or himself in the reading and re-reading of the text and allow the text to explode into every fiber of the human mind and body. This explosion provides what can only be described as a type of spiritual pleasure, a losing oneself in the gripping and groping arms of the text—a "textacy," according to Roland Barthes.[8]

This groping power of the text is akin to how the Old Testament prophet Isaiah speaks and how poet and writer Richard Wright, the Harlem Renaissance phenom, speaks in his epoch-making autobiography *Black Boy*. But more importantly, the spirit of this word, *grope*, as I use it, is captured by the author of the book of Job, who writes, "They grope in the dark without light; he makes them stagger like a drunkard" (12:25 NRSV), and "They meet with darkness in the daytime, and grope at noonday as in the night" (5:14 NRSV). Thus the groping arms of the scripture text should capture and captivate the preacher and raise the sermon to new heights, like the towering strength of the white oak and cedar trees or the sleek, captivating beauty of the towering California redwood.

This groping is the first step in the multifaceted process of getting in front of the text. It is important to emphasize that after reading the text silently to oneself, now the text has to be read aloud, as a type of speaking or speech act. The oralizing of the text is another element in the prelude to understand the scripture text, which is a necessary precondition to explanation in the sermon. Understanding both precedes and follows explanation.[9] In other words, the preacher reads to understand from the very beginning what he or she cannot explain in speech or writing, in the pulpit, or in the public square. This means that the preacher cannot explain that which he or she does not understand. When you interpret yourself, as opposed to understanding yourself, you are always advancing the self in ways that show a lack of self-knowledge. To understand one's self is a journey toward knowing the self. This means that the struggle for self-understanding often escapes our explanation. Explaining looks backward and understanding looks forward. This is prophetic and transforming.

Notes

January

1. Adapted and translated from Hildegard of Bingen's (1098–1179) "O virtus Sapientiae."

2. Elizabeth Boase and Sarah Agnew, "'Whispered in the Sound of Silence': Traumatising the Book of Jonah," *The Bible and Critical Theory* 12, no. 1 (2016): 4–22.

3. Rebecca Lindsay, "Overthrowing Nineveh: Revisiting the City with Postcolonial Imagination," *The Bible and Critical Theory* 12, no. 1 (2016): 49–61.

4. Mark Allan Powell, *Introducing the New Testament: A Historical, Literary, and Theological Survey* (Grand Rapids: Baker Academic, 2018), 141–42.

March

1. Steve Mugglin, "No Condemnation," in *Songs, Lyrics & Stories* (self-pub., 1994), 136, https://www.mugglinworks.com/SongsLyricsStories/SongsLyricsAndStories.pdf.

April

1. James F. McIntire, "Behind Closed Doors" (dramatic monologue sermon, Hope United Methodist Church, Havertown, PA, April 15, 2012).

2. Martin Buber, *I and Thou*, trans. Walter Kaufmann (New York: Charles Scribner's Sons, 1970).

3. George R. Beasley-Murray, *John* (Waco: Word Books, 1989), 70.

4. Joseph Henry Thayer, *A Greek-English Lexicon of the New Testament: Being Grimm's Wilke's Clavis Novi Testamenti* (New York: Harper & Brothers, 1889), 322.

May

1. Ronald J. Allen, "John," in *The Preacher's Bible Handbook*, ed. O. Wesley Allen (Louisville: Westminster John Knox Press, 2019).

2. Jack Levison, *40 Days with the Holy Spirit* (Brewster, MA: Paraclete Press, 2015), 147.

3. Richard Rohr, "Transformation," *Oneing: An Alternative Orthodoxy*, special issue 5, no. 1 (2017): 13.

4. Majorie Hewitt Suchocki, *God, Christ, Church: A Practical Guide to Process Theology* (Chestnut Ridge, NY: Crossroad, 1989).

5. Majorie Hewitt Suchocki, "God, Sexism, and Transformation," in *Reconstructing Christian Theology*, ed. Rebecca S. Chopp and Mark Lewis Taylor (Minneapolis: Augsburg Fortress, 1994), 46.

6. Written by Heather Murray Elkins, copyright © 2001. All rights reserved.

7. Baptismal formula from Riverside Church, New York City, NY.

8. To find out more see the Hispanic Theological Initiative at http://hti .ptsem.edu/.

July

1. Maya Angelou, "On the Pulse of Morning," 1993. This poem was first read at the inauguration of President Bill Clinton.

2. Ernest Hemingway, *A Farwell to Arms* (New York: Scribner, 2014).

3. Bob Vila, "The Plumb Bob," Bob Vila: Tried, True, Trustworthy Home Advice, accessed January 3, 2020, https://www.bobvila.com/articles/495-the -plumb-bob/.

4. Phillip Keller, *A Shepherd Looks at Psalm 23* (Grand Rapids: Zondervan, 2007).

August

1. Fred B. Craddock, "Praying Through Clenched Teeth," in *The Collected Sermons of Fred B. Craddock* (Louisville: Westminster John Knox, 2011), 241.

2. Craddock, "Praying Through Clenched Teeth," 242.

3. Craddock, "Praying Through Clenched Teeth," 242.

October

1. *Daniel Tiger's Neighborhood*, season 4, episode 10, "Daniel's Blueberry Paws/Wow at the Library," aired May 22, 2019, on PBS Kids.

2. Craig A. Evans, "Mark 8:27–16:20" in *Word Biblical Commentary*, ed. Bruce Metzger, David Hubbard, and Glenn W. Barker (Nashville: Thomas Nelson, 2001) 34B:94.

3. Terry Hershy, *This Is the Life: Mindfulness, Finding Grace, and the Power of the Present Moment* (Cincinnati: Franciscan Media, 2019).

4. Eugene Boring, *Mark: A Commentary*, ed. Clifton C. Black, Eugene M. Boring, and John T. Carroll, The New Testament Library (Louisville,: Westminster John Knox Press, 2012), 289.

5. "Leader," Learner's Dictionary, Merriam-Webster, accessed January 3, 2020, http://www.learnersdictionary.com/definition/leader.

6. "Leader," BusinessDictionary, accessed January 3, 2020, http://www.businessdictionary.com/definition/leader.html.

An Advent Sermon: "Like It or Not"—Will Willimon

1. "Like It or Not, God's Redemption" was previously published by Will Willimon in *Crackers and Grape Juice*, December 3, 2018, https://crackersandgrapejuice.com/like-it-or-not-gods-redemption/.

2. Flannery O'Connor, "Wise Blood," in *Flannery O'Connor: Collected Works* (New York: Penguin Books, 1988), 89.

December

1. Deitrich Bonhoeffer, "The Coming of Jesus in Our Midst," in *Watch for the Light: Readings for Advent and Christmas* (Walden, NY: Plough Publishing House, 2001), 201–204.

2. Walter Rauschenbusch, *Christianity and the Social Crisis* (New York: The Macmillan Company, 1913), 345.

3. Based on the tenth canon of the fourth Council of Carthage (c. AD 398).

4. "Sending the Light," copyright © Heather Murray Elkins, 2018. Originally composed for the opening worship of The United Methodist Church General Conference 2019. Included with permission.

5. Frederick Buechner, "Search for a Face," Frederick Buechner Center, accessed January 15, 2020, https://www.frederickbuechner.com/quote-of-the-day/2016/12/24/search-for-a-face. Originally published in *The Hungering Dark* (San Francisco: HarperSanFrancisco, 1969).

Essay: "Play It by Ear"—Talbot Davis

1. This excerpt, "Play It by Ear" by Talbot Davis, is from *Simplify the Message: Multiply the Impact* (Nashville: Abingdon Press, 2020).

2. G. Robert Jacks, *Just Say the Word: Writing for the Ear* (Grand Rapids: Wm. B. Eerdmans Publishing, 1996), 41.

Essay: "Transformational Intellectual"—Richard W. Voelz

1. This excerpt, "Preacher as Transformational Intellectual" by Richard W. Voelz, is from *Preaching to Teach: Inspire People to Think and Act* (Nashville: Abingdon Press, 2019).

2. Gallup Inc., "Sermon Content Is What Appeals Most to Churchgoers," Gallup.com, n.d., http://www.gallup.com/poll/208529/sermon-content-appeals-churchgoers.aspx.

3. Leonora Tubbs Tisdale, *Prophetic Preaching: A Pastoral Approach* (Louisville, KY: Westminster John Knox, 2010), 11–20.

4. Tisdale, *Prophetic Preaching*, 20.

Essay: "Getting in Front"—James Henry Harris

1. This excerpt, "Getting in Front of the Text" by James Henry Harris, is from *Beyond the Tyranny of the Text* (Nashville: Abingdon Press, 2019).

2. Paul Ricoeur, *Interpretation Theory: Discourse and Surplus of Meaning* (Fort Worth: Texas Christian University Press, 1976), 87–88.

3. See Paul Ricoeur, *Hermeneutics and the Human Sciences* (Cambridge: Cambridge University Press, 1981), 15–16. And also John B. Thompson, *Critical Hermeneutics: A Study in the Thought of Paul Ricoeur and Jurgen Habermas* (Cambridge: Cambridge University Press, 1981). Thompson points out the gaps in Ricoeur's claim regarding reference and states, "How a text may disclose a possible world is quite unclear and how one may determine just which world it does disclose remains uncertain" (193).

4. Martin Luther King Jr., *The Essential Martin Luther King Jr.: "I Have a Dream" and Other Great Writings* (Boston: Beacon, 2013), 33.

5. See Paul Ricoeur, "The Model of the Text: Meaningful Action Considered as a Text," *Journal of Social Research* 38, no. 3 (Fall 1971): 534.

6. See Paul Ricoeur, *The Symbolism of Evil* (Boston: Beacon, 1967) and *Interpretation Theory* (Fort Worth: Texas Christian University Press, 1976), 19–22.

7. See Roland Barthes, *The Pleasure of the Text* (New York: Farrar, Straus and Giroux, 1975).

8. See Roland Barthes, "Theory of the Text," in *Untying the Text*, ed. Robert Young (New York: Routledge, 1990), 33.

9. See Ricoeur, *Interpretation Theory*, 71–89.

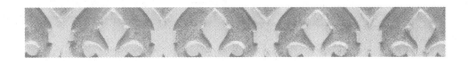

Contributors

Lectionary Sermon and Worship Helps

Sheila M. Beckford—pastor, Wethersfield United Methodist Church, Wethersfield, CT
June 20; August 29; October 24

Tanya Linn Bennett—general editor, *The Abingdon Preaching Annual 2020*; associate dean for vocation and formation, and associate professor in the practice of public theology and vocation, Drew Theological School, Madison, NJ; ordained elder, Greater New Jersey Conference, United Methodist Church
February 28; April 1; April 18; November 28; December 5; December 12; December 19; December 26

Sudarshana Devadhar—resident bishop, New England Conference, United Methodist Church
February 21; May 2; August 1

Drew A. Dyson—ordained United Methodist elder; executive director, Princeton Senior Resource Center, Princeton, NJ
March 14; April 3; August 15

LaTrelle Miller Easterling—resident bishop, Baltimore–Washington Conference, United Methodist Church
May 23; November 21; December 24

Heather Murray Elkins—professor of worship, preaching, and the arts, Drew Theological School and the Graduate Division of Religion, Drew University, Madison, NJ
May 30; December 25

Roslyn Lee—pastor, Commack United Methodist Church, Commack, Long Island, NY
January 17; March 7

Ernest S. Lyght—retired bishop, New York and West Virginia Areas, United Methodist Church
June 13; October 10; November 7

James F. McIntire—pastor, Royersford United Methodist Church, Royersford, PA
April 11; August 8; September 26

Lydia Muñoz—lead pastor, Church of the Open Door, Kennett Square, PA; ordained elder, Eastern Pennsylvania Conference, United Methodist Church
March 25; July 18; November 14

Kirsten S. Oh—professor of practical theology, Azusa Pacific University, Azusa, CA; ordained elder, California Pacific Annual Conference, United Methodist Church
January 24; April 25; October 3

Harriett Olson—chief executive officer, United Methodist Women, New York, NY
July 25

Grace S. Pak—director of cross-racial/cross-cultural leadership, General Commission on Religion and Race, United Methodist Church
February 7; May 9; October 17

Jennifer Pick—pastor, First United Methodist Church, Mexia, TX; Central Texas Conference, United Methodist Church
March 21; April 2; August 22; September 19; November 25

Todd Pick—senior pastor, First United Methodist Church, West, TX; Central Texas Conference, United Methodist Church
March 21; April 2; August 22; September 19; November 25

Jennifer Quigley—assistant professor of New Testament and early Christian studies, Drew Theological School, Madison, NJ
January 3; March 28

Meredith E. Hoxie Schol—director of doctoral studies and assistant professor in the practice of education and leadership, Drew Theological School, Madison, NJ
May 31; October 31

Kathleen Stone—senior pastor, Wharton United Community Church at St. John's, Wharton, NJ
June 6; September 12

Javier A. Viera—dean and professor of pastoral theology, Drew Theological School, Madison, NJ
February 14; May 13; July 4

Will Willimon—professor of the practice of Christian ministry, Duke Divinity School, Durham, NC; retired bishop, North Alabama Conference, United Methodist Church
January 10; April 4

Karyn L. Wiseman—Herman G. Stuempfle Associate Professor of Homiletics, United Lutheran Seminary, Philadelphia, PA; pastor, Gloria Dei Church, Huntingdon Valley, PA
January 31; May 16; June 27

Laurie K. Zelman—ordained deacon, Montville United Methodist Church, Towaco, NJ
February 17; July 11; September 5

Contributors

Essays for Skill-Building

Talbot Davis is pastor of Good Shepherd Church in Charlotte, North Carolina. He has served as a pastor in United Methodist congregations for nearly three decades and is the author of several books, including *Crash Test Dummies* from Abingdon Press.

James Henry Harris is the distinguished professor and chair of homiletics and pastoral theology and research scholar in religion and humanities at the School of Theology at Virginia Union University and pastor of Second Baptist Church (West End), both in Richmond, Virginia.

Richard W. Voelz is assistant professor of preaching and worship at Union Presbyterian Seminary in Richmond, Virginia.

Scripture Index

Online Edition

The Abingdon Preaching Annual 2021 online edition is available by subscription at www.ministrymatters.com.

Abingdon Press is pleased to make available an online edition of *The Abingdon Preaching Annual 2021* as part of our Ministry Matters online community and resources.

Subscribers to our online edition will also have access to preaching content from prior years.

Visit www.ministrymatters.com and click on SUBSCRIBE NOW. From that menu, select "Abingdon Preaching Annual" and follow the prompt to set up an account.

If you have logged into an existing Ministry Matters account, you can subscribe to any of our online resources by simply clicking on MORE SUBSCRIPTIONS and following the prompts.

Please note, your subscription to *The Abingdon Preaching Annual* will be renewed automatically, unless you contact MinistryMatters.com to request a change.